A PLACE OF BELONGING

A PLACE OF BELONGING

FINDING YOUR SPACE IN THE BIBLE,
DURING LENT AND BEYOND

LAVINIA BYRNE

INTELLIGENT ♦ INSPIRATIONAL ♦ INCLUSIVE
SPIRITUAL BOOKS

First published in 2026 by
Darton, Longman and Todd Ltd
Unit 1, The Exchange
6 Scarbrook Road
Croydon CR0 1UH
editorial@darton-longman-todd.co.uk

This product conforms to the requirements of the European Union's
General Product Safety Regulations (GPSR).
EU Authorised Representative for GPSR:
Easy Access System Europe –
Mustamäe tee 50, 10621 Tallinn, Estonia
gpsr.requests@easproject.com

© 2026 Lavinia Byrne

The right of Lavinia Byrne to be identified as the Author of this work
has been asserted in accordance with the Copyright, Designs and
Patents Act 1988.

ISBN: 978-1-917362-14-6

No part of this book may be used or reproduced in any
manner for the purpose of training artificial intelligence
technologies or systems.

A catalogue record for this book is available from the British Library.

Designed and produced by Judy Linard

Printed and bound in Great Britain by Ashford Colour Ltd

Contents

	Introduction	7
1	A Gathering of Gardens	13
2	Scaling the Heights	29
3	A Mountain too Far?	45
4	Inhabiting the City Wall	61
5	Inside the Whale – Lessons of the Deep	77
6	Beside the Well	95
7	The Fiery Furnace – A Double Whammy	113
8	All at Sea	133
9	The Heavens are Telling	149
	Acknowledgments	168

Introduction

The meaning of Lent

Lent has a single focus and makes singular demands. It invites us to think about the place of suffering in our lives and how we can find meaning in it.

It holds up the example of Jesus and asks us to explore what the Bible has to say about his search for meaning.

Above all it is a time to receive. There is so much happening in our lives and all around us that tries to ensnare us, to depress us and pull us down. How helpful to be offered a slice of time that can help us to evaluate, reappraise and emerge strengthened into the light.

This book links this special time, its strengthening and light, with a very definite set of places. In each of these we can experience our own humanity and learn more about ourselves. In each of these we can receive the gift of God.

How do we know this to be true? Each is a place, but also a space. Here an encounter has already taken place, one recorded in the Bible and reflected on down the generations. By slowing down and choosing to inhabit this space, we can draw wisdom from it. Our reflections take root and help us deal with the world around us and the countless demands made on our time and energy. It can help us become more thoughtful and open to receive the true graces of the season.

A Place of Belonging

Where to begin?

Where do you feel most at home? Where do you belong? Most of us have an answer to those questions and draw comfort from the security that comes when we have a named place of belonging. Equally, many of us know how painful it is to be displaced. To be place- or home-less is a fate we would not wish on anyone. As millions of people are becoming displaced from their homes and beginning a heart-breaking quest for a new land or shelter, our newspapers and TV screens bring their plight into immediate focus. Wars and rumours of wars abound. Land grabs are the order of the day. All of a sudden the issue of place or space has become intensely topical.

Time to engage with powerful ideas such as who belongs where, how we all fit, what we can do to ensure there is room for everyone. Our thoughts and feelings about territorial rights and about migration/immigration cannot be left in the hands of politicians or economists. By taking responsibility for our own sense of place we engage with questions that have far-reaching effects on the lives of other people.

Yet place is a wider concept than simply 'home'; it can mean a situation or state of mind. We aspire to be in a 'good' space and spend time and energy devising strategies to get there.

How useful then to examine a collection of places that have been valuable and important to other people. How helpful to be able to develop a vocabulary to describe the places in which we find ourselves; to analyse how we fit in; what works for us. To discover where and how we belong.

Introduction

Seeking wisdom

This book examines a sequence of places that have worked for historical people whose stories have been preserved so that we can learn from them. A sequence of spaces where human beings like us have struggled to work out their true identity: where they have discovered who they are, and who they are in relation to other people.

They have situated themselves – and so may we.

The source I have used to find these archetypal places is the Bible. I could so easily have turned to Greek and Roman mythology, or to medieval literature, or even to Shakespeare. I could have ransacked poetry or song lyrics – even contemporary ones – because the themes of belonging and not belonging, of loving and being loved are universal and ever present. Instead, I have deliberately chosen a source which is available to anyone with an enquiring mind. I am aware that the Bible comes with baggage, which makes reading it critically both challenging and fun. The discovery involved in stripping away tiers of pious interpretation reveals a text that is both passionate and illuminating by turns. Like an archaeologist, you can dig down and find layer upon layer of treasures and meaning. The secret is to dispense with all your preconceptions, to let go of your bias and to become a true explorer.

The characters who people the pages of the Bible are a thoroughly motley crew. They get into incredible scrapes and muddle through. They are mean and kind by turns, heroic and pitiful, magnificent and cowardly. Every adjective applicable to human behaviour can be applied to the saints and sinners whose stories are narrated here.

Interestingly their stories happen in time and space. Above all space. The whole thrust of the Scriptures is toward manifestation or revelation. Quite evidently the ultimate story they tell is that God made human beings and our world. In the Christian imagination the final act comes when this history is brought to a fine point: the birth of a baby in a manger. Jesus is born in a defined place and in a defined time. Theologians call this moment the incarnation.

Where to develop and grow

This book seeks to explore some of the other places in which human beings are offered insight and wisdom because they too can have a theological interpretation, and this clarification opens windows in our imaginations. We can all benefit from the call of the mountains, or the ocean wave. These are nice places, but human growth happens in the dark as well as the light. For this reason, we need to consider the belly of the whale and the fiery furnace too: difficult places where you may not feel at home; places where you have no desire to dwell.

The word dwell is critical. It sounds vaguely old-fashioned, even a bit primitive. A dwelling, after all, might be akin to a hovel. Yet it could be a palace. What I have discovered by reflecting on a variety of biblical places is that all that matters is the quality of the experience, the actual act of inhabiting the situation in which we find ourselves, in order to draw benefit from it. And, if necessary, to move on.

The places in this book are places of belonging – and also discovery. They accommodate you however or whatever you are feeling. They offer you resonance and hospitality – even the uncomfortable ones – because they are places where people like you have experimented and

Introduction

looked for meaning. That is why they are worth exploring.

When we are prepared to reflect on our own experience, we enhance our choices, giving them added value when we understand and interpret them. This book advocates a transitory approach to human living rather than a static one, recognising that we like trying out new experiences before acting on them.

If you read it carefully, you will find you can understand your own preferences and interpret them. Eventually you can exercise some control over where you choose to dwell. Above all, you will learn to inhabit each stage of your personal journey with authority and with hope.

How does the Bible fit?

I believe that the Bible as a source book for human understanding must submit to interrogation: we must read it intelligently. This book is written with that conviction and, ideally, it too will reward careful reading.

Moreover, if you are a believer, even a troubled believer, it will lead you to a space where you will enjoy a deeper encounter with yourself and ultimately – if that is what you are looking for – with God.

A Place of Belonging

How to use this book

Either on your own – or together if you belong to a prayer or reflection group – choose to read it chapter by chapter, taking time to think about what you read.

You may even decide to write something down after you have completed the exercises at the end of each of them, or copy out the prayers for your own use.

In this way you will produce a journal of your own personal reactions so that you have a record to treasure as you approach Holy Week and Easter. For some people drawing a picture is even more important than writing down words. Choose what suits you best.

Don't worry if you haven't finished by any particular deadline. It is more important to take your time and enjoy the journey, than to arrive at a given destination.

The value of working with the text is to deepen your own experience of belonging.

Chapter 1
A Gathering of Gardens

Introduction

Ancient literature, old books, old stories all know about gardens and the power of gardening. Gardens represent beauty, and somehow, we have always known that nothing beats growing something and seeing life flourish in the little world of seed and soil, sun and water. This is hardly surprising because from its first beginnings, human life has had a context. The one provided by the earliest creation story in the Bible is a garden. We know it as the Garden of Eden.

This is the first of the gardens to be considered in this gathering. What do they have in common? They are all places where we are offered understanding and wisdom in an almost elemental form. Places where you can elect to find yourself, if you so choose.

Multiple creation narratives

Creation stories abound in Mesopotamian literature so, interestingly, we find at least two different ones in the Bible. The one given in Genesis chapter one has God taking seven days over creation. The order is significant: on day one, we hear the magnificent words, 'Let there be light', with the astonishing and instantaneous reaction: 'And there was light' (Gen. 1:3). With the gift of light comes clarity, vision and a host of expectations. This makes it the ultimate gift.

What is clear from this account is that the author is not remotely interested in scientific accuracy or in how God created everything. This is why he claims that light was created before the source of light, namely the sun. What interests the author of Genesis chapter one is the powerful contention that God created everything. And that God was pleased with everything created and found it very good. Not in how it was made, but why it was made, and what that means for us. In this account, the sun and moon were not made until day four. The initial gift is of light and it comes with an offer of illumination and of understanding.

There is no Garden of Eden in this story, rather the whole of created reality becomes a vast cradle for the generation of humanity, with human beings seen as the very peak of creation. They are created 'in the image of God, male and female' (Gen. 1:27). Human destiny is secure, because it is bathed in light and has the capacity to offer illumination to all that is made. This it does by mirroring and reflecting the divine radiance. Light is more than a lone beam: it dances and bounces around: 'And it was very good' (Gen. 1:31).

The Story
Human life begins in a garden

In the story given in Genesis chapter 2, the scene is more intimate. And it is set in a garden. In this case creation happens in a single day: 'the Lord God formed man of dust from the ground and breathed life into his nostrils and man became a living thing' (Gen. 2:7). No sun, no moon, no swirling stars. Simply a garden. But what a garden: the most luxurious and fertile place imaginable. This is because, we are told, we were all given a place when God created a garden for us, 'with every tree that is pleasant to sight and good for food' (Gen. 2:9).

The double purpose of this garden is immediately established. It is to be aesthetically pleasing – a feast for the eyes and other senses, especially we may assume, smell – but also a literal feast, namely a source of food. Four rivers irrigate the garden, including the Tigris and the Euphrates, so the resources are there for it to flourish. God gives the man a task: he is 'to till the garden of Eden and keep it' (Gen. 2:15). A deliberate connection is made: the man came from the dust of the earth, and he is charged with caring for it. He is to work the land so that it can bring forth fruit.

The little clay mannequin is given life directly from the breath of God and he is given a vocation: he is to become a gardener.

Who is missing?

But something is not quite right. Our narrator realises his account is incomplete, so he has God cast about for what is missing. After all, there is something wrong with this idyllic garden. Where are the animals, the slugs and snails obviously, but also the robin that sits on our spade, the dog that buries its bone? So 'the Lord God formed every beast of the field and every bird of the air and brought them to the man to see what he could call them, and whatever the man called every living creature, that was its name' (Gen. 2:19).

A Place of Belonging

There is absolutely nothing scientific about this account so to use it to condemn the theory of evolution, as some have tried to do, is totally to miss the point. A metaphorical language is being used to describe a different kind of evolution altogether, that of a network of relationships where every living being has a place. In the garden of Eden everyone belongs. There are no insiders or outsiders.

Only, of course, there is still a massive hole in the divine canvas. The man has still not found 'a helper fit for him'. Where is the woman without whom this magnificent garden and all the living creatures and teeming life who make up its eco-system are somehow inconsequential? Without the woman, no new human life can be generated. Extinction of the human species threatens before the whole thing has properly begun.

Our author becomes inventive; he takes control of the narrative. After all, every good story demands a bit of magic:

> So the Lord God caused a deep sleep to fall upon the man, and he slept; then he took one of his ribs and closed up its place with flesh. And the rib that the Lord God had taken from the man he made into a woman and brought her to the man. Then the man said,
>
> > 'This at last is bone of my bones
> > and flesh of my flesh;
> > this one shall be called Woman,
> > for out of Man this one was taken.'

> Therefore a man leaves his father and his mother and clings to his wife, and they become one flesh. And the man and his wife were both naked, and were not ashamed.
>
> (Gen. 2:21-25)

The narrative is complete. Woman, man, birds, animals are all set for a story that must have a happy ending, for what this account sets out to describe is surely paradise? The garden is a place of belonging, a place where love and life can flourish in equal measure and, in the words of Julian of Norwich, 'all shall be well'.

'The Fall'

Our narrator is not naive: he has to explain the dissonance between the dream landscape he conjures up here and the angry reality of human life as he experiences it all around him. For that reason, he has to use certain dramatic conceits to make sense of lived human reality.

He has to invent a villain, to introduce a couple of hurdles which will prove treacherous for the enchanted couple he has brought into being. He needs to account for human behaviour, the human condition. At this point we too have a task because we in turn need to dig deeper and to find out what biblical commentators have to offer to explain what is going on. The Bible demands interpretation and explanation. Scholars date this account of creation to the time of King David and King Solomon – namely some 1000 years before the Christian era and light years later than the time it purports to describe. Context is all and it dictates many of the features of this narrative. Our author wants to write about the very origins of the human family, but he also has several points to make.

First things first, modern commentators give this author a name. He is called the Yahwist and known as J because he uses the name YHVH or Lord God to tell his story. He is also called the Jahwist, which is the German spelling of the word with essentially the same pronunciation. Hence the letter J. The author of the other, or seven-day account of creation is likewise given a name: he is called P, representing the Priestly source and his or, more probably, their account is from the fifth century BCE, so from a later period of history.

The lessons of biblical scholarship

When he casts about for ideas to elaborate his account, the Yahwist does not have far to look. The central plank in his narrative is critical: God made the original couple in the safety of the paradise he has dreamed up. He is convinced they were made to till the earth and help it bring forth fruit and produce. He wants us to understand that all human life comes from this perfect crucible, that the garden he depicts is both the source of their very being – after all, they come from clay – as well as their destiny. Everything they need is there: they inhabit an earthly paradise. Even the Lord God, their maker, chooses to walk there in the cool of the evening.

So what could possibly have gone wrong? Our author has his ear to the ground. He knows that all is not well in the world he actually inhabits. The people of Israel have enemies and our author's king, the former shepherd boy David, has to defeat them if he is to have any traction. Philistines, Moabites and Ammonites have to be conquered and, above all, to be integrated into the life of the kingdom.

A Gathering of Gardens

How powerful to produce an account of creation which demonstrates that all tribes, all nations have one set of parents – and one set only. We belong to each other.

But what about evil? How to explain the origins of sin? Again, our author casts about in his known world to explain what is happening. He thinks about a known arena of transgression: he remembers how a woman – as he saw it – drove King David into adultery and then murder. When Bathsheba took a bath on a rooftop that overlooked the king's palace, she became an instrument in his downfall. David fell for her, slept with her, she conceived and lost his child, he had her husband killed, he acted in ways that brought his reputation into disrepute. His destiny was sealed.

The author of Genesis chapter two had a ready-made scenario which he could transport into the Garden of Eden. Think of a man, a golden, illustrious model human being. Cast him as Adam. Then think of a woman, a sinful temptress, a Bathsheba. Call her Eve. But he still needed a total villain, a character who could insinuate himself into the heart of the story. Enter the serpent. Where did our narrator find the evil snake? Again, he looked around at the known world formed by his own circumstances. No creatures were more evil, as he understood things, than the snakes, the serpents which were used in temple worship by the pagan forces who opposed David and the Israelites.

A ready-made cast of characters were placed centre stage for the next twist in the creation plot. The story has been told and re-told: about a tree with a forbidden fruit, about how a serpent tempted Eve and 'she did eat', about how the woman led the man astray and 'he did eat', about how the Lord God took action and they were cast out of the garden. About how clothes were made for them, and they embarked on life outside the Garden. About the condition of humanity later described by Milton as Paradise Lost. Namely how the golden couple were condemned to leave the garden as a result of their pride and disobedience.

The Wisdom

Why is any of this important? Only when you understand where these creation stories come from can you let them speak with any authority to present-day reality. To dismiss them as fairy tales, or to rubbish them as unscientific is to miss the point entirely.

The abundant Gardens of Eden

The Garden of Eden is the starting point for a whole sequence of mythological meanings. In literature and art, creative people have revelled in giving us their interpretations. From Dante to Arthur Miller, from Hieronymus Bosch to Rubens, via Michelangelo's Sistine Chapel, poets, playwrights and artists have striven to depict its glories. The results are stunning: depictions of nature at its most voluptuous and fruitful; an Adam and Eve surrounded by enchanting animals; peace, harmony – and then, in the corner, that niggling, creepy, slimy adversary, the serpent.

Yet arguably none of these depictions on canvas or in words has been more powerful than the physical reality of the real thing, as it were. Persian enclosed or paradise gardens began to flourish during the time of the Achaemenid rulers, namely the sixth century BCE. Visitors to Iran can still see these ornamented gardens in cities such as Yadz and Shiraz. Acres of fig trees, pomegranates, vines, orange trees and above all roses transform a landscape, offering a visual but also a scented feast.

The main feature of these ancient gardens is their use of water to form pools, flowing streams, cascades. These have so many purposes: to transport water to all the living plants and foliage, obviously. Above all – and this is not incidental – to provide a soundscape, for nothing is more evocative than the sound of water, falling, dripping, rippling, manifestly alive. Equally, when it stands still in pools, nothing is more effective as a mirror to capture reflections of the sky, to bring it, quite literally, down to earth. Unsurprisingly gardens were adopted by Islam too and the Quran is as insistent as the Bible: 'Allah has promised to the believing men and the believing women gardens, beneath which rivers flow, to abide in them, and goodly dwellings in gardens of perpetual abode; and best of all is Allah's goodly pleasure; that is the grand achievement' (Quran 9.72).

Until you travel in the near east, the word garden probably summons up something green, a space that is orderly and disorderly by turns. True gardens in the biblical understanding are more like deserts to a European reading of the text. That is why the account in Genesis 2 is so refreshing: it represents a true oasis, a place where air, water, light and vegetation meet. A place where you can enjoy shade, relief from the power of the sun. A place of encounter. So, even here, the predominant colour is green. This is not by chance for the colour green has a large part to play in the paradise experience.

Green is a composite colour, a blend of blue and yellow, and nature is skilled at blending it in a myriad of ways through generating chlorophyll. This means green is not static: it is a dancing colour, capturing energy from light and transforming it into growth. No wonder we associate green with hope and new life; no wonder we feel happy when exposed to new ideas – green shoots in our thinking.

Time to move on, to leave the enchanted garden and explore some other green shoots.

Other biblical gardens – the night-time garden of pain

This is because there are other gardens to explore in the pages of the Bible. All of them are evocative of the highs and lows of human experience. Each of them is a place for us to visit to enhance our own sense of values and meaning. Take, for example, the Garden of Gethsemane where Jesus went to pray before his arrest. This garden in east Jerusalem is a place of pilgrimage nowadays. Standing at the foot of the Mount of Olives, it has some of the most ancient olive trees in the world growing in serried rows, with dusty soil, gnarled roots and scrub bushes half-exposed to the light.

This is remembered as a garden of shame, where Jesus' apostles slept whilst he contemplated his approaching death and fought to submit to it as an expression of God's will for him. A place of blame too, where Judas brought soldiers to arrest him and delivered the kiss that identified their victim. Shame and blame are hard to acknowledge, and even harder to cast off. Yet the only way to deal with them is to recognise them and then let them go.

The events of Jesus' arrest take place in the dark. That kiss was needed to identify the transgressor, to isolate and single him out from a group of men huddled around him. What an irony that both the kiss and its recipient carry meanings which convey the opposite of what would have been the case in daylight. A kiss is ordinarily a mark of love, not of betrayal; the transgressor, in this instance, was an innocent man. In a darkened garden, anything becomes possible. All our values become inverted, and we begin to make colossal mistakes.

In the account given in John's Gospel, these mistakes are highlighted and interpreted through the interplay of light and dark. When his disciple, Judas, left the final meal Jesus shared with his friends, they imagined he was off to do some good deed, to 'give something to the poor'. Instead, he was going to the authorities with the intention of having Jesus arrested and tried – and all for his paltry reward of thirty pieces of silver. John's comment is chilling: 'And it was night' (Jn. 13:30). The dark most feared by followers of the light descended and embraced them all. The dénouement would follow in the Garden of Gethsemane. No wonder it stands in such bitter contrast to the first, the original garden where, seemingly, only light prevailed.

The garden of revelation

Another garden, and one of hope and exultation this time: the Garden of the Resurrection where his disciple Mary Magdalene discovered Jesus disguised as a gardener, beside an empty tomb. This is a garden of transformation, where despair is turned to hope, desperation to glory. The story is told in John's Gospel chapter 20 and describes how Jesus appears to Mary after his resurrection.

The actual site of this garden is hard to identify. Golgotha – or Calvary as it is known in Latin versions of the Bible – was a place outside the wall of the city of Jerusalem where criminals were executed. Difficult to imagine that sorry identity nowadays when visitors see the magnificent Basilica of the Holy Sepulchre which has been built on the alleged site. Originally conceived by the Emperor Constantine, it was placed on the spot where his mother Helena was supposed to have found remnants of the cross on which Jesus died. Subsequently the original building was destroyed during the Crusades and then restored. Its massive presence nowadays is so resolutely a million miles away from any garden that a huge effort of the imagination is required to look for a simple landscape beyond the imposing, if very beautiful, basilica.

Yet such an imaginative leap is just what is required if we are to rediscover some of the innocence of that original encounter. We do not know what it means to rise from the dead; we do not know what it means to discover an empty tomb. Yet so much of Christianity's vast edifice – so similar to the Basilica of the Holy Sepulchre – is predicated on this luminous meeting. Which is why it repays investigation. Beyond the demands of scholarship, beyond the superstructures we impose on reality, there is something deeply simple to visit and to revisit. Ideally with the eyes and ears of a gardener.

The gardener, after all, knows all about life after apparent death, about seasonality, about the return of hope where there was none.

The final garden
The last book of the Bible takes us back to the beginning. The holy city, the new Jerusalem comes down from heaven. All right it is a city, but it has a river where the

water of life flows like crystal. 'On either side of the river is the tree of life with its twelve kinds of fruit, producing its fruit each month; and the leaves of the tree are for the healing of the nations' (Rev. 22:2). Mysteriously this tree of life represents the reconciliation of human history and, so with T. S. Eliot, we can say, 'In my beginning is my end', and conclude by knowing, 'In my end is my beginning' (*Four Quartets* Part II: 'East Coker', line 1). Or, to put it another way, 'The fire and the rose are one' (*Four Quartets* Part IV: 'Little Gidding', final line).

There is an enchanting circularity when you engage with planting and growing things: the seed that falls into the ground becomes a plant that generates further seeds; the cuttings plunged into pot of water grow wavy roots; the weeds that, once weeded, spring up again inexorably. And somehow, beguilingly, what is predicted here is healing. The 'healing of the nations'.

Discovering your own garden

So far four archetypal gardens have emerged: the original garden, the garden of pain, the garden of revelation and the heavenly garden of ultimate healing. Then there are gardens that can flourish in our imaginations as well as physically in reality, or in the pages of a book such as, in this case, the Bible. And these are the gardens that we in turn can create.

These gardens are places to cultivate, places to escape to. Gardens of discovery, of pain, of disclosure and of healing. The life of the human spirit becomes a source of exploration that can be as fruitful as the original Garden of Eden, if only we take care to let it grow.

Ask any gardener what qualities they develop as they

get stuck in and you will find they list attributes that have a direct application in the interior world where our gardens of disclosure also flourish. Chief among these is the virtue of patience. Time itself gets re-configured when subjected to the deeper rhythms imposed by the seasons of planting, growth and reaping a harvest. There is no point trying to hurry a process on when it happens so slowly as to be imperceptible.

Add to that the virtue of trust. Anyone who has ever planted a seed knows how astonishing it is when this tiny scrap of life starts to grow in the dark and then reveals itself when it is ready. The gardener can only hope, and by some miracle this hope gradually deepens and becomes trust when the green shoots appear.

Finally, there is the extraordinary leap of joy that comes from tending something that actively flourishes. The miracle of growth is mediated so very directly when represented by green shoots. God or, if you prefer, nature is at work here and always present to it. No wonder that the gift of a garden, or a planet brings with it a commission. With privilege comes responsibility. The charge is to look on the land with the gaze of God. Beyond any sense of entitlement is the commandment to take care of the earth, as God desires, within the rhythms of nature.

Becoming a gardener

To end with reality: our Biblical destiny as gardeners is one most of us live out with extraordinary interest and pleasure. Even those of us who have never linked the cultivation of our window box or sprawling flower beds with the story of creation. Gardening is essentially creative and that has to be why it is enjoyable. To make something out of nothing; to bring colour where there was none; to nurture something as tiny as a seed and see it turn into a living plant: each of these activities answers a deep need in the human spirit.

As gardeners we become creators; as gardeners, we transform the planet or at least our small patch of it. No wonder the idea that human life began in a garden is so attractive. Even the Priestly author tells us that human beings are made in the image and likeness of God, here portrayed as the ultimate gardener.

We pray to God the gardener:
Open our hearts to find your will for us.
May we grow in the sure knowledge that you are our
beginning and will be our end.
Help us to put down deep roots, and to grow according to
your plan for us.
This Lent, help us to belong to you. Amen.

Action

- This Lent, why not grow something? Take a photo of it on day one, even if it is a seed hidden in a pot.

- Visit a cherished garden and apply each of your senses to discovering what it is trying to tell you about your vocation as a gardener. Look, listen, touch, smell and, ideally, taste your way round this garden. If there is some water, try looking at the reflections it captures, including one of yourself if you can. Is there any shade? Slow down, breathe deeply and enjoy the total experience of being in this garden. Can you give it a name?

- What do you do to cultivate the life of your spirit? Imagine you are in your own personal garden, taking a look at your own personal life. What qualities do you want to see flourishing there? Write down three of them.

- How do you cope with pain or betrayal? How do you nurture hope? There is no right or wrong answer. Simply acknowledge that they are part of what it is to be human and to be alive.

- What can you do to help promote the 'healing of the nations'?

- Think about the opposite of a gardener. What name would you give to the sense of entitlement that leads some to see land only in terms of acquisition, conquest and exploitation?

Chapter 2
Scaling the Heights

Introduction

When did you last have a peak experience? This is usually interpreted as something that happens in our minds or spirits. The fantastic glow that lights us up when we see someone we love, or hear music we enjoy, or achieve something special.

But what about the idea of going up in the world or making it to the top? A plethora of metaphors in English come from the language of climbing, scaling, reaching the heights. In so many aspects of our lives there is a hidden drive to get on – which means onwards and upwards.

When you physically climb a mountain there are lots of pluses: first, the vision you get when you are up high enough to have a panoramic view of your surroundings. This offers a change of perspective when you see how tiny things look when viewed from above. What loomed large when you were below it is relativised and loses some of its importance. Even its threat and possibly its charm. Then there is the clean air you breathe when you rise above normal levels of pollution. This can be a heady experience, bringing clarity and freedom as you breathe in fresh oxygen. Above all, there is the sense of achievement

A Place of Belonging

– for every climb demands a physical and emotional effort. And the rewards are massive.

In reality though, we know that mountains can be treacherous places. The difficulties and dangers of mountain climbing are well known, and most of us lack the nerve as well as the opportunity to take the obvious risks. But even as armchair mountain climbers – as it were – we can experience the lure of mountaineering; we can revel in the imagery and leave to other people the feat of getting to the top.

Unlocking the imagery

This mixture of intense pleasure and jeopardy explains some of the lure of aiming for the heights. I am old enough to remember the excitement of what was called the conquest of Everest. On 29 May 1953, the explorer Edmund Hillary and the Sherpa, Tenzing Norgay, climbed the South Col route up the world's highest mountain. The date is significant because two days later the news of the success of this British-led expedition reached London – on the morning of the coronation of Queen Elizabeth II. I cannot have been the only small child to have confused these events in my mind. They were both about elevation and triumph and genuine excitement. Inevitably we played a game in the garden at home called 'Climbing Mount Everest'. It involved scrambling up an old gate which had been leaned against a stone wall, and when/if I got to the top, I was convinced I would be crowned Queen.

Somehow, the sense of achievement that successful mountaineering represents draws us in. We aspire to experience the sense of surpassing ourselves, as well as other people. How helpful to turn to other explorers of different mountains knowing they can offer us the wisdom they learned there. They too have touched the pleasure and the pain that go with their mountaintop encounters.

There are a bewildering number of mountains in the Bible story. The names are evocative: Sinai, Hebron, Tabor, Carmel, Moriah, Zion. All are recognised as places where something important happened, but drill down and a pattern emerges, a pattern that can be explored and explained.

The Story

To interpret the mountain experience, it helps to attach a human name and story to each of these biblical settings. In that way we can situate ourselves relative to them because they become embodied in the story of the individuals who climbed them.

Abraham and Mount Moriah

This is a mountain of trial and of pain, but also of revelation. A mountain where an important transaction takes place and religious practice gets turned on its head. The old man Abraham was given a cruel task. According to Genesis chapter 22, he was commanded by God to take his son Isaac up Mount Moriah and to kill him. Brutally, he was told to sacrifice his beloved son, Isaac, his first-born child, his only chance of being father of a great nation.

Abraham could be described as the oldest real person in the Bible, in the sense that the account of his life is set in real time. He is described as the true father of his people or patriarch and, although his personal existence cannot be corroborated from sources outside the Bible, the internal evidence stands up to scrutiny. There was a group of people known as 'Apiru' or Hebrews; there were known customs such as having a child by a servant – as was the case with Isaac's half-brother Ishmael; the name Abram has an actual meaning, namely 'God is exalted'. This indicates that the context that gave rise to his story can be verified. But it is what happened on the mountain top that makes the account of the transformation enacted there so sensational. This trauma is unique to the Book of Genesis; it enters the history of ideas through this particular route.

Understand how the story of Abraham is narrated, understand this sorry scene on Mount Moriah, and you have a key to understanding the whole of biblical literature. It is always about more than what you read on the page; it always requires analysis and interpretation.

And this, of course means that readers must be honest about their motivation. Do you want to be a fundamentalist, dedicated to defending the literal truth of every word you read in the Bible because your own belief system is predicated on this? Do you want to be forensic, because you believe that, like any other piece of literature, its stories can be better understood when contextualised and carefully studied? Or do you want to rubbish it because you think too much damage has been done to humankind in the name of the beliefs and behaviour apparently advocated in its pages?

Revisiting the Bronze Age

For the forensic reader, it is useful to go back 4000 years and see what is going on. The story of Abraham is set in the middle Bronze Age, so people have learnt how to blend tin and hot copper to make artefacts of considerable artistic value, as well as cups and plates and forks and spoons. They can write and draw up lists; they have learnt how to travel and to trade; they are budding scientists and are developing belief systems to explain the workings of the universe. They can also make knives.

At a place called Ur of the Chaldees – in present-day southern Iraq – we are told that a young man called Abram embarked on an immense journey, as he set off for Haran in modern Turkey. A physical journey, but also a spiritual one because, once there, he had to abandon the worship of the deity practised in Ur – a moon god called Nanna – and embrace the Lord God, YHWH. This transformation from what can loosely be called paganism to the worship of a single God – or monotheism – is a milestone event in the development of the human spirit. In the person of Abraham, a revolution was set in motion.

Moon worship is totally understandable, indeed attractive. The moon is so very real and so important for its role in human and animal fertility. To worship the moon is to be in touch with growth, to imitate its patterns of waxing and waning. Moonlight transforms a landscape, offers a fresh way of looking at things and appears to offer wisdom. Small wonder that moon worship is a worldwide phenomenon and that it certainly passed from Sumerian or Mesopotamian practice into the Greek and Roman worlds. The goddesses Artemis and Diana testify to that. The Greek worship of Artemis highlighted her role as moon goddess and this was transferred across and adopted by the Romans when they too took over her cult and re-named her Diana.

But the choices made by the young Abram when he set off on his travels brought him to an emotional crossroads, marking a transition from the pagan world where things from nature were turned into deities, to a spiritual world where ideas could float free. Such a dramatic change did not happen in an instant. It required a re-booting of his entire consciousness, and this would take a great stretch of time and many different experiences to bed down in his understanding. The story of how Abram became Abraham as told in the Bible is essentially the story of this spiritual journey.

Sustained by the promise that he would become father of a great nation and accompanied by his wife Sarai, he left Haran and set off on further travels to the land of Canaan. Several journeys later, a rich man now with a nephew, Lot and with Ishmael, the son born by his wife's slave woman Hagar, Abram settled down to enjoy his old age. But a further surprise awaited him: not only did God want to single him out and make a covenant with him, giving him the new name of Abraham, but three visitors appeared at the door of his tent with a blinding promise. Abraham and his wife, now called Sarah, were to have a son of their own. His new name even had a new meaning: 'father to generations of offspring'.

The birth of a miracle boy

The text tells us that Abraham was 99 years old when this happened, a neat way of suggesting how improbable and spectacular this birth would be. Remember that we are in biblical territory where myth and historical reality weave a narrative pattern that is more interested in meaning than in factual accuracy. This is where biblical scholarship can protect us from the naivety of literalism.

The miracle boy, Isaac, was duly born and so we can

fast forward to the fateful day when the Lord God spoke to Abraham again: 'Take your son, your only son Isaac, whom you love, and go to the land of Moriah, and offer him there as a burnt offering upon one of the mountains of which I shall tell you' (Gen. 22:2).

Our author, the source called J, because he calls the Lord God YHWH, spares no details. He has the aged patriarch set off for the mountain, cut wood for the burnt offering and, after three days travel, bind his son with ropes. We are told that 'Abraham put forth his hand and took the knife to slay his son' (Gen. 22:10) when an angel of the Lord intervened. A ram whose horns were caught in a thicket replaced Isaac and was offered as a burnt sacrifice in his place.

This story is distressing on so many levels: what kind of a God demands the sacrifice of a child? What kind of a father would take a knife to his son's throat? How on earth can a dynasty be generated when the mountain of Moriah is so nearly a place of carnage? A place where dreams are shattered. Unravel the story and a fascinating step forward in human understanding is revealed.

What is this story about?

The story of Abraham was written down some 1500 years after it was supposed to have taken place. A lot had happened to the patriarch's descendants in the interim and that is why the tale is related the way it is. Our author has an agenda. On one level he wants to emphasise how wonderfully the Lord God deals with the chosen people, with those who fulfil the divine will, however impossible that seems. Using a degree of hyperbole, he wants to make a political point: Abraham is the father of his people, and his story is the most ancient story possible. Like the mountain top, much of the detail is shrouded both from view and from human understanding, but the patriarch Abraham is exemplary, and his behaviour cannot be faulted.

The political reality does nothing to take away from the drama of that moment on the mountainside when something intolerable was asked of the old man, not only the death of his son but the crushing of his dream. His hopes and fears were laid bare, and yet he demonstrated that he was willing to let everything go in the name of a higher good – as he saw it. Few of us face such a momentous crunch time; but many of us have to let go of ambitions and dreams.

How helpful to discover that the thicket on a mountainside can provide a substitute and that we can live to fight another day. Even when we are faced with impossibility and with ultimate tragedy, this story promises us another way forward. Traditionally this is how the event on Mount Moriah has been interpreted. The boy Isaac was free to come down the mountain with his father and to carry the old man's dynastic hopes into the future. God offered a substitute, a ram which was duly sacrificed, and life could go on.

What is really happening?

But the real psychodrama of the Abraham story is that something brand new is offered to the human spirit on that mountain top. Whereas Abraham went up the mountain with his head still full of the old way of doing things – burdened, quite literally, with firewood and a knife, all the paraphernalia of human sacrifice – he came down the mountain knowing that God did not want that of him. God had no desire to see him sacrifice his son, to be bound by the old way, which was all about appeasement and wrath and bloodletting. Archaeological evidence has been discovered demonstrating that human sacrifice, particularly of children, was the norm in primitive belief systems and certainly practised in Ur of the Chaldees. And yet here we have a story that shows God actively repudiating such a thing.

Mount Moriah tested Abraham's ability to let go of the past and all its certainties and embrace the new future he had been offered with the revelation that YHWH was more than a moon god. From now on, he was safe to cast off pagan practices and rejoice in a new way of doing things. Mount Moriah was the final hurdle, the ultimate test, and when Abraham reached into the bush and grabbed the ram by its horns, he demonstrated his own liberation – along with that of his son, Isaac. The thicket gave way and yielded up its own offering.

A journey up Mount Moriah becomes the offer of something radical and something new. Despite the pain of letting go, and the appalling drama of killing a child, it carries an invitation: to let go of our certainties – and embrace a different perspective. In religious language, to let God be God. In human language, to let ourselves evolve and be prepared to start again: to change our preconceptions.

Moses and Sinai
Interestingly this second biblical story is set on a different mountain. Our hero is no longer Abraham with his dynastic ambitions and his endless journeys in pursuit of a land. Instead of the patriarch, we have a lawgiver, Moses,

and a whole other way of looking at the history of this emerging people. Our author this time is drawing on a variety of sources, but he too is interpreting these through a grid, a network of meaning: he too has a point to make.

Rather than attributing all the promises of the relationship God has with this particular tribe back to primitive times, to the pre-history represented by Abraham and his family, he wants to update and to localise these to make his point. That is why his focus becomes the mountain where God reveals the Ten Commandments, namely Mount Sinai.

Traditionally and throughout ancient history, mountains have been seen as the habitat of the gods, of divine beings of every kind. Mount Olympus is familiar in the western world as the home of Zeus, and both Greek and Roman myths abound with mountain stories. Sacred mountains feature in eastern mystical writings and folk tales too as abodes of the gods – places where they live, or where they can hide or even get up to mischief. In the Bible, God does not live on a given mountain; rather all mountains are part of the divine creation and manifest celestial strength. Sinai stands out because God chose to be known there.

This mountain of disclosure becomes a turning point in the lives of the allies who had followed Moses – along with his brother Aaron and sister Miriam – out of Egypt. This is where Moses' identity as founder of the Jewish faith is sealed. For this reason, scholars have tried to give a date to this momentous event. The year 1250 BCE seems to be preferred for the story of how the Israelites left the land of Egypt where they had been held as slaves.

Scaling the Heights

An Iron Age tale

This places the Exodus firmly in time at the start of the Iron Age. Civilisation is moving forward at a pace as artisans begin the mass production of a lighter, more durable metal than bronze. Tools became easier to work with which meant that agriculture could flourish in new ways, people could feel more secure about where their food was coming from and, if they chose to settle in larger communities, they could protect themselves more effectively. No wonder the Ten Commandments engage with the protection of what is mine and what is yours, and that they legislate for the use of animals and possessions as well as human relations. They reflect the society from which they emerged.

So much for the historical context the authors of the Book of Exodus were grappling with. When was their book written and what difference does this make? Scholars suggest that a finalised version of the first five books of the Bible can be dated to as late as the fifth or fourth centuries BCE. This means that, once again, there is a huge gap between the actual events they describe and their capture on a written page. Arguably the Book of Exodus is as much a creation story as the two given at the start of the Bible, in the Book of Genesis. Only this time, instead of taking the Garden of Eden as its starting point, it takes Mount Sinai. To our authors the gift of the Law is as important as the gift of life.

A pattern for living under God's law

This book was written by people who believed passionately that the ordering of their lives in the light and sight of God's teachings secured their eternal destiny.

A Place of Belonging

The covenant God made with Moses found expression in teaching which became sacred, and which was to be observed in every particular. The Ten Commandments blossomed into myriad rulings that covered every aspect of human living and brought it under the loving gaze of a God who was deemed to be interested and concerned about every single thing. Pattern secured meaning and keeping the patterns or rules equated to personal and corporate integrity.

Turn to Mount Sinai and see what it has to teach us today. Here we have a mountain of disclosure, a sacred place where God came down and spoke with a mere mortal, with Moses. A bit of a comedown to discover that we cannot actually physically turn to this mountain because no one knows exactly where it is. Somewhere in the Sinai Peninsula, to the very south of Israel, there are various candidates for this sacred role. The actual site remains a mystery.

God comes to the mountain

What happened there is depicted as equally mysterious. The Book of Exodus has a fully theatrical account of the meeting with God that took place on Mount Sinai. There is a name for this explosive display of power and majesty and might in natural phenomena. It is called a theophany, namely an event where the presence of the divine is revealed within created reality. Rather like the performance of a magisterial piece of music on the organ, all the stops are pulled out and nature roars out a great blast of sound and an explosion of light.

Scaling the Heights

> On the morning of the third day there was thunder and lightning, as well as a thick cloud on the mountain, and a blast of a trumpet so loud that all the people who were in the camp trembled. Moses brought the people out of the camp to meet God. They took their stand at the foot of the mountain. Now Mount Sinai was wrapped in smoke, because the Lord had descended upon it in fire; the smoke went up like the smoke of a kiln, while the whole mountain shook violently. As the blast of the trumpet grew louder and louder, Moses would speak and God would answer him in thunder. When the Lord descended upon Mount Sinai, to the top of the mountain, the Lord summoned Moses to the top of the mountain, and Moses went up.
> (Ex. 19:16-20)

What does all this mean for us? There is an encounter. It is marvellous beyond anything Moses has experienced so far. High up on a mountain top, everything changes for him. He sees with new clarity and understands what is being asked of him in a totally new way. The God who is revealed to Moses is utterly transcendent, other, beyond anything he had known up until that moment. He could have felt devastated. Yet what God offered Moses was not fragmentation or destruction, rather, in the gift of the Law, he was given purpose and structure. The 'smoke of the kiln' turned out to give him a shape and form whereby he and his friends, his nation could find harmony and meaning.

We too are offered encounters if we displace ourselves and take the risk of travelling away from what is familiar to us. The mountains on offer to us may not be anything like so considerable as Sinai was to Moses, but there is a promise here. Try to work out what motivates you, what rules you live by, what attitudes you hold dear, and see if there is room for growth, for changing your mind, for opening your heart to new insights and ways of doing things. Risk an encounter with your inner being and see where you are led. You might find a new pattern, a new way of proceeding. The Sinai story shows how such physical and emotional displacement can bring us to a new place with new rules, new ways of operating. You might not even want to go there and there is always an element of risk in going up a mountain, but that is the whole point.

Once again, a mountain-top story offers the promise of a new vision, a new start. A development in our own integrity.

The Wisdom

How do we pull together the wisdom revealed in these geographical locations and the experiences they offer in a way that has some meaning nowadays?

Just as the garden stories offered us a new role for understanding ourselves and our own motivation, so too these mountain-top tales bring us insight and wisdom.

With Abraham we go on a journey; we develop a family and network of relationships; we grow prosperous and garner experiences; we sort out our priorities and we come to the mountain top with definite certainties and discover it is a place of pain because something immense is demanded of us. Out of the blue a hurdle appears. But it turns out to be an immense liberation because we realise that our previous perceptions have been transformed. We are offered a new way of proceeding and even the God we think we have understood and either worshipped or discarded is re-configured.

With Moses we are offered the security of re-creation: by recognising there is a code, we learn the way forward into adult life. The gift of the law is far more than a list of dos and don'ts; it is a portal into respectful living with our fellow human beings and the whole of created reality. Above all there is a proposal here: about embracing integrity and truthfulness and having these as core values. Up the mountain we are offered time to evaluate our own commandments and see if they are fit for purpose or simply a list of prejudices and worn-out clichés. In the clear air we can take a deep breath and start again.

The stories of Abraham and of Moses operate at the level of ideas and not simple events. Genuine revelation is transformative because it enables us to change our minds as well as what we do. Put simply, we are both challenged and re-motivated, or even re-calibrated, by what we learn on the mountain top.

We pray to the God of revelation,
show yourself to us as you are, not as we fear you to be;
show us the way up the mountain of truth and joy and enlightenment.
Help us to treasure your will for us.
Make us good and happy, this day and evermore.
This Lent, help us to belong to you.
Amen.

A Place of Belonging

Action

- Think of the most important moments in your life. What important thing did you learn about yourself as you reflect on what they meant to you?

- Can you give a 'tag' or strap line to your mountain? Was it a moment of pain or disclosure or discovery?

- If you were embarking on a fresh experience right now, who would you take with you? Who would be your ideal mountaineering companions? What commandments would you hope to discover? And what criteria would they be based on? Would they help you become kinder? More loving? More truthful?

- 'When I was a child, I spoke as a child, I felt as a child, I thought as a child: now that I have grown up, I have put away childish things' (1 Cor. 13:11). Can you let go of the understanding of God, of religion you were brought up with? Can you let faith grow in you?

- This Lent, as you think about the suffering and death of Jesus, remember that he went willingly towards the moment of pain. His Father too was not a vengeful God, out for human blood. Rather the pattern and order he had set up led to an extraordinary revelation: the triumph of love, of 'laying down your life for your friends' (Jn. 15:13).

Chapter 3
A Mountain too Far?

Introduction

A peak experience offers transformation – to your beliefs, as in the case of Abraham – but also to your behaviour, as became clear when Moses received the commandments. The stories told about mountain-tops recognise the need for change, for the kind of makeover that is more than skin deep. They are inevitably about encounters, essential transforming meetings. With God, evidently, because of the nature of the text. This, after all is the Bible and it has a major role in trying to help us understand how religious belief takes root and grows in people. But also and always it is about meeting yourself – and this happens best when you are in an especially undefended and vulnerable state.

To go up the mountain is to allow yourself to have a brand-new experience, unmediated by anything you are comfortable with, and delivered to you by unfamiliar elements. The peak experience gives you a unique understanding of the human condition. You cannot escape from yourself as you become exposed to your own humanity. You are alone with your own hopes and fears and angels and demons. You are undefended because there is no one to pretend to and suddenly you realise you cannot deceive yourself.

That is what the climbers in this chapter discovered when they risked the adventure of going up a mountain.

The Story
Elijah and Mount Horeb

With this story we come to a totally different kind of theophany from the fully orchestrated one described in the Book of Exodus. The mountain this time is called Horeb, which is an alternative name for Mount Sinai. Same mountain as for the revelation of the law, but a different experience is on offer. Rather than the fireworks version of divine intervention, we have here the 'small still voice' that is probably more familiar to most of us, though equally transforming. Either way, something new is shown to us and our perspective changes; once again the mountain top works its magic and offers a further insight.

The story is told in the First Book of Kings and it is set on the Sinai Peninsula. The prophet Elijah came to hide here after a tempestuous encounter with the prophets of the pagan god, Baal. The mountain is called Horeb because the narrator of this particular story used a source called by the same name as the Bible's Book of Deuteronomy. That is why the author — or most likely authors — are known as D. In the two books they compiled, called the Books of Kings, they covered centuries-worth of history and some of the materials they used may in fact belong close to the events they describe. Scholars reckon the complete text was written down in the sixth century BCE. But the Elijah story is set well before that. What does this mean? Principally that this is not an eye-witness account.

A Mountain too Far

The context

Elijah's story begins some three hundred years earlier. The Stone, Bronze and Iron Ages have each contributed to the development of technology. The move now is away from discovering and using materials to trading in them. Small ships used the seaboard coast of the Levant to go in one direction, out west towards the Mediterranean countries and beyond. Meanwhile camel trains set off southwards across the Arabian deserts in another. The small nation under Jewish shepherd kings such as David was perfectly positioned at the intersection where these trade routes crossed. Their seaboard neighbours in Tyre and Sidon in particular enjoyed prominence. These great Phoenician ports supplied the west with luxury goods coloured with the purple dye for which they were renowned. At the same time incense from Oman made its way into the temples of what would become the Greek and Roman gods. And imports such as tin from Cornwall filled the empty boats on their return east.

With the interchange of goods, fresh ideas too began to circulate. The cults of gods and goddesses supply evidence of an exciting cultural melting pot. In time the Greek gods Zeus and Hera would re-materialise as their Roman counterparts, Jupiter and Juno. Such shapeshifting had occurred earlier when the deities of the Levant, Baal or Melquart of Tyre became Herakles and Ashtart, the queen of heaven equated to Aphrodite. When people travelled and traded, their belief systems came along with them, as well as the paraphernalia of temples and statues and priests and sacrifices. The possibilities for exchanging ideas along with goods were endless and paralleled what was going on in the little seaside ports and market squares around the known world. Ideas proliferated – and fizzed.

With such an explosive pantheon of gods so readily available, how remarkable that monotheism as expressed in the religious beliefs of the Israelites ever survived. After all, polytheism was so deeply attractive: it offered a deity for every occasion, a friend, an ally for every cause. Squabbles between the gods and the attitudes they struck mirrored human behaviour. They served as examples and role models. They helped people understand human nature precisely because they so often represented the projections of real live human beings. No wonder they became archetypes and Greek dramatists eventually wrote their plays to be performed in their honour.

How Elijah fits in

Chief among the defenders of monotheism was our prophet, Elijah. He lived in stirring times, the ninth century BCE to be exact. His whole life was dedicated to overthrowing the pagan god Baal and proving that his own ineffable and invisible Lord was more than a match for this manufactured idol. As he would have seen it, Baal was a human construct – though even Elijah had to recognise that he was none the less powerful for all that. The point about Baal was that he was everything an agricultural community would want their god to be. He was in charge of fertility which made him the supreme force within nature as he also controlled rainfall and the distribution of storms. To the agricultural nations of the ancient near east, he was the deity most to be feared because he secured their prosperity along with the wellbeing of their fields and flocks. The cult of Baal was widespread and inevitably

A Mountain too Far

Elijah, as prophet of the Most High, took up arms against this most intransigent of gods.

To defend the name and identity of Lord God, he set up a competition on yet another mountain: Carmel in the north of the country. Here two bulls were prepared for sacrifice and Elijah taunted the 450 prophets of Baal who assembled to oversee the operation. The account is gruesome and triumphalist by turns.

> They took the bull that was given them, prepared it, and called on the name of Baal from morning until noon, crying, 'O Baal, answer us!' But there was no voice, and no answer. They limped about the altar that they had made. At noon Elijah mocked them, saying, 'Cry aloud! Surely he is a god; either he is meditating, or he has wandered away, or he is on a journey, or perhaps he is asleep and must be awakened.' Then they cried aloud and, as was their custom, they cut themselves with swords and lances until the blood gushed out over them. As midday passed, they raved on until the time of the offering of the oblation, but there was no voice, no answer, and no response. Then Elijah said to all the people, 'Come closer to me'; and all the people came closer to him. First he repaired the altar of the Lord that had been thrown down; Elijah took twelve stones, according to the number of the tribes of the sons of Jacob, to whom the word of the Lord came, saying, 'Israel shall be your name'; with the stones he built an altar in the name of the Lord. Then he made a trench around the altar, large enough to contain two measures of seed. Next he put the wood in order, cut the bull in

pieces, and laid it on the wood. He said, 'Fill four jars with water and pour it on the burnt offering and on the wood.' Then he said, 'Do it a second time'; and they did it a second time. Again he said, 'Do it a third time'; and they did it a third time, so that the water ran all around the altar, and filled the trench also with water. At the time of the offering of the oblation, the prophet Elijah came near and said, 'O Lord, God of Abraham, Isaac, and Israel, let it be known this day that you are God in Israel, that I am your servant, and that I have done all these things at your bidding. Answer me, O Lord, answer me, so that this people may know that you, O Lord, are God, and that you have turned their hearts back.' Then the fire of the Lord fell and consumed the burnt offering, the wood, the stones, and the dust, and even licked up the water that was in the trench. When all the people saw it, they fell on their faces and said, 'The Lord indeed is God; the Lord indeed is God.' Elijah said to them, 'Seize the prophets of Baal; do not let one of them escape.' Then they seized them; and Elijah brought them down to the Wadi Kishon, and killed them there.

(1 Kings 18:26–40)

This account gives Elijah a decisive victory. He is shown to be devout and mocking by turns, and then downright vindictive. He appears not to have a doubting bone in his body. Like many a zealot, he is an absolutist with no compunction. What mattered was strength – and winning, albeit in the name of his God. A terrifying formula and one which has led to so much evil and destruction in human society. All in the name of religion.

A Mountain too Far

The mature Elijah

It is with some relief that we turn to the encounter on Mount Horeb. Here we find an exhausted prophet who drags himself up the mountain after all the tumultuous events that have characterised his service of the Lord up to this point. Here is a man who really could do without any more divine instructions, especially if they are intended to call him to further exploits.

Go up Mount Horeb with him and what do you find? The account in 1 Kings 19 is revelatory:

> The word of the Lord said, 'Go out and stand on the mountain before the Lord, for the Lord is about to pass by.' Now there was a great wind, so strong that it was splitting mountains and breaking rocks in pieces before the Lord, but the Lord was not in the wind; and after the wind an earthquake, but the Lord was not in the earthquake; and after the earthquake a fire, but the Lord was not in the fire; and after the fire a sound of sheer silence. When Elijah heard it, he wrapped his face in his mantle and went out and stood at the entrance of the cave. Then there came a voice to him that said, 'What are you doing here, Elijah?'
>
> (1 Kings 19:11-13)

This event has famously been recalled in the words of 'Dear Lord and Father of Mankind', a hymn by an American Quaker, John Greenleaf Whittier (1807-1892). The meaning of Elijah's encounter is distilled in the verse:

> Breathe through the heats of our desire
> thy coolness and thy balm;

> let sense be dumb, let flesh retire;
> speak through the earthquake, wind and fire,
> O still, small voice of calm!

At last, something benign is on offer. In the gentle murmur of the still, small voice, Elijah can let go of his grandiose posturing and find meaning in the trivial, the mundane. He can let go of the big, large-scale events of his earlier life and be ordinary. Of course, there are further tasks to be done. For a start he must anoint his successor, Elisha. But basically, he can unwind. He may be able to come down from the mountain and begin to cultivate his own garden.

This makes Mount Horeb a mountain of discovery. The showmanship is over and with Elijah we can relax into a whole new way of approaching life. With him we too can paint on a smaller canvas and find pleasure in little things, discern the lighter strokes by which truth is revealed to us, and learn not to be afraid of our own frailties. We too can learn to listen to the still, small voice within.

The concern here is with maturity. On Mount Horeb, Elijah discovers something different. Whereas he had thought that the worship of God was all about bombast and a triumphant display of how right he was to promulgate his own vision and beliefs, on the mountain he learns ease and directness. God comes to him in the simplest of forms, the mountain breeze.

You need to be very sensitive to feel such a gentle stimulus. It helps if you can be open to the idea that there is more in the life ahead of you than there has been in the life behind you. The future holds out a promise. You may safely come down the mountain and begin your life all over again. On Mount Horeb, Elijah is offered a fresh start, one which promises to be bring coolness, and even the healing power of balm.

Jesus and Mount Tabor

One more mountain and this time from the New Testament, that part of the Bible where there is no longer a centuries-wide gap between the events being described and the account given in the written narratives or gospels. An eyewitness or even a participant most likely contributed to how this story is told.

The Tabor experience

Jesus goes up a mountain with three of his friends: Peter, James and John. All three of the Synoptic Gospel writers, namely Matthew, Mark and Luke take up the story. Here goes for Mark's account, chosen because Mark supposedly relied on Peter for his version of events.

> Six days later, Jesus took with him Peter and James and John, and led them up a high mountain apart, by themselves. And he was transfigured before them, and his clothes became dazzling white, such as no one on earth could bleach them. And there appeared to them Elijah with Moses, who were talking with Jesus. Then Peter said to Jesus, 'Rabbi, it is good for us to be here; let us make three dwellings, one for you, one for Moses, and one for Elijah.' He did not know what to say, for they were terrified. Then a cloud overshadowed them, and from the cloud there came a voice, 'This is my

A Place of Belonging

> Son, the Beloved; listen to him!' Suddenly when they looked around, they saw no one with them anymore, but only Jesus.
>
> (Mark 9:2-8)

Mark gives short versions of his stories, offering the barest of details – which makes his text especially interesting to unpick. This is his account of what has come to be known as the Transfiguration.

It is the only story in the Bible where Jesus himself becomes the object of a miracle. Ordinarily signs such as these happen to other people. Here he is with his closest friends – Peter, the first of the men he chose to follow him; and the brothers, James and John, also fishermen from Lake Galilee. Tradition gives the location as Mount Tabor, now known as a place of pilgrimage, called the Mount of the Transfiguration. Once again there has been a church on the site since the fourth century – at first a Byzantine basilica, then a Crusader church and now, acting out the vagaries of history in stone, a Franciscan monastery sprawling over the landscape.

Jesus is shown to be in conversation with the lawmaker, Moses, and a leading prophet, namely our friend Elijah. His clothes shine with bright light and the event becomes a theophany. This means that the existence of God suddenly became known to them in the most direct way possible. All the classic ingredients are here: the light, the cloud, the utter terror, and then the voice. God is on display on the mountain, wanting to be known. No wonder Peter reacts as he does: how to enshrine the moment, to turn the vision into an event? He suggests that they should build three little huts so that each of the transfigured figures should have a proper place to dwell. He wants to make sure everyone has a home.

What he experiences is so utterly normal that it becomes reassuring. In the face of something so wonderful and yet so bewildering, what could be more natural than to try to capture the event and make it last? Our own peak experiences can be as transitory, and we know all too well how much we would like to hold on to them and turn them into more than memories. And nowadays, in the age of TikTok and Instagram, nothing feels more natural, more normal than to whip out your phone. The instant video is only a click away.

Time to listen

A kind of induction is going on here. The voice uses words that have already been heard in the Bible's account of Jesus' life. At his baptism in the river Jordan, again in the account given by Mark, we read, 'In those days Jesus came from Nazareth of Galilee and was baptized by John in the Jordan. And just as he was coming up out of the water, he saw the heavens torn apart and the Spirit descending like a dove on him. And a voice came from heaven, "You are my Son, the Beloved; with you I am well pleased".' (Mk. 1:9-10).

There is a significant difference between the two accounts. At the river Jordan, the voice had offered an acknowledgment; here, on the mountain, there is an admonition: 'Listen to him'. And when they look around, they see no one anymore. Except they do; they see Jesus and their focus is now directed only to him. To seeing him and to listening to him. Their vocation is sealed.

A double transfiguration takes place. Not only is Jesus

newly affirmed and refocussed on his teaching, preaching and healing mission, but Peter, James and John are also transfigured. They too, as a result of this encounter on the mountain, can step forward with new confidence. They are on the way to becoming apostles.

Only, of course, they are also the frail and unreliable men Jesus will take with him into the Garden of Gethsemane, where they fall fast asleep. The transfiguration takes time to bed down. Encouraging news really: our peak experiences, those times when we know for certain who we are and where we are going in life can prove horribly illusory. It is quite hard to keep seeing and keep listening, even when we have had the most transfiguring of confirmations.

The Wisdom

With Elijah, we discover the secret that lies beyond the showy display of earthquake, wind, and fire. We learn about the value of peace, of calm of the 'still small voice' that starts life as a gentle murmur, whatever our age, and ends as the insistent accompaniment to our later years when we in any case have to slow down and take stock.

With Peter, James and John we go up the mountain of the transfiguration in the full knowledge that our own attitudes and preconceptions can be transformed. But, once again, we realise such transfiguration is a lifetime's work.

Every peak, every mountain top offers a different experience; it is up to us to decipher their meaning and bring this meaning down with us to bear fruit in everyday living. And of course, coming down the mountain is difficult because it might mean losing something, namely the raw quality of the meeting we had there. It might mean finding our own self is anything but transfigured, that we too will fall asleep in the garden of need.

The reassurance of these biblical accounts is that there is life beyond the mountain-top experiences; the instantaneous event – the reveal or disclosure – can take a lifetime to unpack. The only mistake we could make would be to try to stay on the mountain or, with Peter, to try to make the experience cosy by building a little hut up there. To try to make the experience last by protecting it from the crushing experience of real life. Genuine transfiguration has to be tested, as the Bible in fact knows. In all our lives there will be earthquake, wind and even the drama of fire. And beyond all that, the delicate breeze of ongoing conversion, of change, of alteration, of becoming.

We pray to the God of transformation.
Help us Lord, to become more open to finding our true
selves and to discovering you. Lead us up your holy
mountain and bring us down again safely.
Transform us. Help us become more open to the gentle
influence of your divine will.
This Lent, help us belong to you. Amen.

Action

- Take time out. Go to a mountain top inside your head and explore what is on offer there. Can you strip out the different elements and influences you could describe as tumultuous, rowdy and dangerous; as earthquake, wind and fire? Do you dare discern something smaller and quieter at work there. Listen to its messages.

- The life described by the Rule of St Benedict is predicated on the idea of 'conversion of manners', of repeatedly doing things over and over so that you become the person you want to be. What kind of a person would you like to be and what characteristics in your personality would you like to develop?

- Who do you most trust? The person who is always right – especially when it comes to art, or culture, or religion, or politics, or someone who is an explorer, able to change their mind and open to transformation. Which would you rather be? Are you free enough to look again?

- Where are you tempted to build little huts? To put barriers up round what you hold most dear, to institutionalise? Try saying these words from Psalm 121: 1-8.

  I lift up my eyes to the hills— from where will my
     help come?
  My help comes from the Lord, who made heaven
     and earth.
  He will not let your foot be moved; he who
     keeps you will not slumber.
  He who keeps Israel will neither slumber nor
     sleep.

A Mountain too Far

> The Lord is your keeper; the Lord is your shade
>   at your right hand.
> The sun shall not strike you by day, nor the
>   moon by night.
> The Lord will keep you from all evil; he will
>   keep your life.
> The Lord will keep your going out and your
>   coming in from this time on and forevermore.

- Do you find it difficult to forgive yourself? To start again? This Lent, why not offer yourself a personal transfiguration? Take time to listen to the frailest and smallest of voices that you hear.

Chapter 4
Inhabiting the City Wall

Introduction

How well defended are you? Have you ever felt defenceless or wondered where to turn for protection or help? Have you ever felt you were under siege and that your resources were running low? Have you ever longed to escape from a relationship or a situation and wondered how on earth to break free? Have you ever gazed beyond the known and the familiar and longed for something more than what you have and know?

How strange, after enjoying the freedom offered us within nature, to find ourselves drawn to think about shelter; to reflect on a structure that appears to be designed to keep wild things at bay. Why think about the wall built around a city to protect it and the people who live within it? Why dream of life both within and beyond the gleaming spires?

On a wider canvas – and thinking beyond how well or badly defended we may feel in our own personal lives – there is the broader question of city or country walls. Most famously there looms the wall proposed between North America and Mexico. This has been presented as a solution to all the USA's issues with immigration from the south. Ditto the watery wall that would descend in the English Channel, were it possible to 'Stop the Boats or 'Smash the Gangs'.

Along with these physical walls there are the closed minds and attitudes that surround so many of our mental citadels: the impregnable values we claim to hold dear; the intransigent attitudes that make dialogue impossible. I remember seeing a slogan written on a wall in Paris when I went there in June 1968: '*Attention, les oreilles ont des murs*' – 'Watch out: ears have walls'. Alongside the cobblestones torn out of the streets by rebelling students in May that year, the evidence of unrest contained an emotional and psychological warning too, captured in an image everyone could understand.

A city wall changes meaning depending on whether you are standing inside it and it is protecting you, the people you love and all your interests, or not. If you are safely on the inside, it contributes to your sense of belonging and sets up a positive vibe for you. Stand outside the city wall and your perspective changes. The well-defended city shuts you out; it makes you feel you do not belong, and you have no role in what happens there.

But stand on the city wall, or even – if you are lucky – live in one of the little houses or rooms that have evolved within its fabric and you have a fantastic perspective. You can face inwards and enjoy the rich cultural and emotional life that goes with being a citizen. But equally you can face outwards and be open to wider cultural and political interests.

Think of human skin – the largest of all our organs – and you can see the parallels. A rich organic life flourishes within and our physical being is protected by this amazing living, flexible, waterproof and infinitely vulnerable covering. When we are unwell, our symptoms manifest there; when we age, it reminds us to take care of ourselves. Uniquely it enables us to face in two directions at once, inwards but also outwards towards our past, present and future as real live human beings. We inhabit it and want to be comfortable in it. It is the ultimate membrane, a treasure we share in the most intimate of human activities, when we communicate by touch.

The Story
What skin is to an individual, a city wall can be to a community. Is this why the Bible understands walls? Because its stories are concerned about the well-being both of individuals but also the whole community. In its case the binding force that brings them together is a shared faith and value system. This means belief in a God who calls both individuals and whole nations to live under scrutiny and to be accountable for how they behave towards other people. In any case a history book that stretches as far back as the Bronze Age must surely have wall-shaped wisdom to be studied and unlocked. While age may not always be a guarantee of wisdom, it has its own integrity and secrets to unpack.

The city that lost its wall
Intriguingly the most famous of biblical cities is the one whose walls came tumbling down. So much for building up our sense of security. If anything, it reminds us that even the best fortifications can let us down. We know this place as Jericho, one of the most ancient cities in the world. We may even have sung the jaunty spiritual about the exploits

of Joshua and the battle he fought there. Visit it now and what will you find? An archaeological site called Tell es-Sultan just north of the Dead Sea. And, just up the road, a refugee camp, because this is and has, for many years, been contested territory. With a population of some four and a half thousand people, of whom 81 per cent were refugees in 2018, according to a census conducted by the Palestinian Government, this fragment of terrain on the West Bank of the River Jordan acts as a microcosm for the study of an exceptionally chequered history.

This is a city we visit as outsiders or invaders because we are indeed in the company of Joshua. He was Moses' successor, and the origins of some of this conflicted history are laid out in his story. Joshua had left Egypt with Moses, had wandered through the wilderness with him and now – with the death of his mentor – was set to lead the people against the Canaanites and possess the land he was sure God meant for them. The promise is crystal clear:

> 'My servant Moses is dead. Now proceed to cross the Jordan, you and all this people, into the land that I am giving to them, to the Israelites. Every place that the sole of your foot will tread upon I have given to you, as I promised to Moses. From the wilderness and the Lebanon as far as the great river, the river Euphrates, all the land of the Hittites, to the Great Sea in the west shall be your territory. No one shall be able to stand against you all the days of your life. As I was with Moses, so I will be with you; I will not fail you or forsake you. Be strong and courageous; for you shall put this people in possession of the land that I swore to their ancestors to give them.' (Jos. 1:2-6)

Inhabiting the City Wall

Fortified with such powerful battle orders and totally confident in the righteousness of his cause, Joshua crossed the Jordan and advanced on Jericho. His tactics were sneaky to say the least. The actual siege of the city was a piece of theatre: for six days he had his soldiers march round and round the sturdy walls, with seven priests blowing on trumpets of rams' horns and creating a nightmare din. The desired result came on the final day: 'As soon as the people heard the sound of the trumpets, they raised a great shout, and the wall fell down flat; so the people charged straight ahead into the city and captured it. Then they devoted to destruction by the edge of the sword all in the city, both men and women, young and old, oxen, sheep, and donkeys.' (Jos. 6:20-21)

Strategically speaking, Joshua now had access to key trade routes, going both east to west but also north to south. The road was open for the Israelites to advance in every direction. Unbeknownst to these early campaigners, the goal of the city that would become Jerusalem gleamed just ahead and was suddenly in reach.

Did these events really happen? Most probably not, but what we have here is a powerful piece of propaganda and, yet again, the story was written down long after the events it is supposed to describe. Some five hundred or so years later. The author's intention is to show that the land of Israel is a gift from God and the Israelites received it directly through the heroism of Joshua. The magical words, 'land of Israel', '*eretz Israel*' retain their power because of the nature of the promise and the power of these myths. They have all the force of the early creation stories because, yet again, they are trying to explain the exceptional status of this chosen people as the elect of

God from their earliest origins. And here the message has a double imperative because it demonstrates that what God really intended was not simply a Chosen People but also a Chosen Land, fortified by imaginative boundaries as tight and impregnable as any city walls.

A nice irony then that the story of the conquest of the land begins with an account of walls that crumble. A lightbulb moment, surely, demonstrating that even the best-laid plans can fail, or at least need re-interpretation. Yet what we are meant to learn from this account is that the walls of the most ancient of cities, of the stronghold of Jericho, are powerless against the divine will and against the patriotic din of priestly trumpets. No wonder this colourful story has iconic status. No wonder that, to this day, there are refugee camps and far worse to prove Israeli supremacy and the power of what is perceived to be God's promise to his chosen people.

Rahab the harlot

There is a coda to the Jericho story. Before the siege of the city, a woman called Rahab lived there. Hers was a strategic position: she lived neither within nor without, but actually inside the wall. When Joshua sent a couple of spies to check out the fortifications before he invaded, they ended up staying overnight in her home. This was before the marching around and the shouting and trumpet blasts set in. For some unknown reason she was aware that they were up to no good, but she had an advantage: she was well versed in the history of their people. Her welcome reads like a profession of faith in the one true God, as they would have seen it.

The Book of Joshua takes up the story:

Inhabiting the City Wall

So they went, and entered the house of a prostitute whose name was Rahab, and spent the night there. The king of Jericho was told, 'Some Israelites have come here tonight to search out the land'. Then the king of Jericho sent orders to Rahab, 'Bring out the men who have come to you, who entered your house, for they have come only to search out the whole land'. But the woman took the two men and hid them. Then she said, 'True, the men came to me, but I did not know where they came from. And when it was time to close the gate at dark, the men went out. Where the men went, I do not know. Pursue them quickly, for you can overtake them.' She had, however, brought them up to the roof and hidden them with the stalks of flax that she had laid out on the roof. So the men pursued them on the way to the Jordan as far as the fords. As soon as the pursuers had gone out, the gate was shut.

Before they went to sleep, she came up to them on the roof and said to the men: 'I know that the Lord has given you the land, and that dread of you has fallen on us, and that all the inhabitants of the land melt in fear before you. For we have heard how the Lord dried up the water of the Red Sea before you when you came out of Egypt, and what you did to the two kings of the Amorites that were beyond the Jordan, to Sihon and Og, whom you utterly destroyed. As soon as we heard it, our hearts melted, and there was no courage left in any of us because of you. The Lord your God is indeed God in heaven above and on earth below. Now then, since I have dealt kindly with you, swear to me by the Lord that

A Place of Belonging

you in turn will deal kindly with my family. Give me a sign of good faith that you will spare my father and mother, my brothers and sisters, and all who belong to them, and deliver our lives from death.' The men said to her, 'Our life for yours! If you do not tell this business of ours, then we will deal kindly and faithfully with you when the Lord gives us the land.' Then she let them down by a rope through the window, for her house was on the outer side of the city wall and she resided within the wall itself. She said to them, 'Go toward the hill country, so that the pursuers may not come upon you. Hide yourselves there three days, until the pursuers have returned; then afterward you may go your way.' The men said to her, 'We will be released from this oath that you have made us swear to you if we invade the land and you do not tie this crimson cord in the window through which you let us down, and you do not gather into your house your father and mother, your brothers, and all your family. If any of you go out of the doors of your house into the street, they shall be responsible for their own death, and we shall be innocent; but if a hand is laid upon any who are with you in the house, we shall bear the responsibility for their death. But if you tell this business of ours, then we shall be released from this oath that you made us swear to you.' She said, 'According to your words, so be it.' She sent them away and they departed. Then she tied the crimson cord in the window. (Jos. 2:2-21).

The ploy worked. The men made their getaway and, when the wall eventually fell, Rahab and all her family were saved. The dangling red cord saved them. And the position of Rahab's house gains in meaning. We are told that 'she resided within the wall itself'. Her privileged position gave her access to the inner and outer worlds of conquering and conquered and she created a bond between the two. This story might seem to be of no consequence – even though it makes Rahab the patron saint of all sex workers – were it not for two further scriptural references to this woman.

Rahab in history

She crops up again in the most implausible of contexts. In the first chapter of Matthew's Gospel, in what is known as his genealogy, there is a list of all Jesus' forebears going right back to Abraham. And there she is: 'Rahab who became the mother of Boaz', a direct ancestor of king David – and so of Jesus.

Evidently it pays off to occupy a house on the battlements and to have an eye open for the main chance when an invading army is on a collision course with your city. Contemporary feminism loves this story. It places Rahab the prostitute along with three other women who are also mentioned in this list. The first is Tamar, portrayed quite inaccurately as another good-time girl – who 'seduced' her father-in-law Judah, and produced twins, which was always considered a great move in patriarchal circles. Another reading of her story would suggest that she was raped by Judah and was only given a name in history or celebrity status because she produced male offspring. Just as well that recent feminist scholarship has totally dismantled these portrayals, restoring agency to the female players by revealing the patriarchal bias of the narrative.

A Place of Belonging

Next up is the virtuous Ruth the Moabite, the foreigner who sought out her husband Boaz 'amid the alien corn', as the tender image in John Keats 'Ode to a Nightingale' would have it. Encouraged by her mother-in-law Naomi, this young widow threw in her lot with her former husband's people and converted to their religion. Her reward: her place in the lineage of King David, her great-grandson.

The next woman in the list is not graced with a name, but simply referred to as Uriah's widow. We know her as Bathsheba, celebrated for her visits to the bathing pool that lay in direct line of vision to the rooftop where King David was wont to stroll of an evening. The reader could be forgiven for seeing in her another trophy hunter because of the way the story is narrated. The political bias of this account is self-evident – and totally unapologetic.

Predictably the final woman in this list sparkles with an unblemished record and is free of any of these historic associations: Mary, 'of whom Jesus was born, who is called Christ' (Mt.1:16). She enters left field, apparently with no ancestors and is identified by 'Joseph the husband of Mary', whose ancestors have just been detailed.

A strange story of spies and hiding in city walls and being lowered by a rope and the auspicious red ribbon of salvation ends in a birth that is predicted to be redemptive for the whole world.

Martin Luther's 'Letter of Straw'

The other biblical reference to Rahab and her home on the city wall comes in the Letter of James, a relatively obscure text in the New Testament. One of the earliest pieces of Christian writings, this Letter is concerned with practical things, like what to do with your money and how to speak wisely and control your tongue. James has a good word for – of all people – Rahab, praising her for her 'good works'. One person who did not like this interpretation one little bit was Martin Luther who, overseeing the birth of Protestantism and concerned to demonstrate the supremacy of faith over works, tried to have the Letter thrown out of the Bible, calling it a 'Letter of Straw'.

The text remains – and with it, the good name of Rahab the harlot: 'Likewise, was not Rahab the prostitute also justified by works when she welcomed the messengers and sent them out by another road? For just as the body without the spirit is dead, so faith without works is also dead' (Ja. 2:25-26). In other words, a curious memory of salvation at the hands of a stranger turns out to have a meaning that extends far beyond the incident itself. The historical resonances of our actions are incalculable. In the case of Rahab, she made use of the wall that was her home so that it faced inwards, protecting her and her family, her clients and her neighbourhood, but also outwards so that it offered salvation to her enemies. And, in the event, this ability to look beyond the walls secured her own survival as well. In a strange way, the wall mirrored the levels of exposure she experienced both in her professional life – facing outwards – and her personal life – facing inwards.

The holy city of Jerusalem

The greatest of all cities for the people of the Bible is Jerusalem. In a way, it is also the ultimate mountain as it is built on Mount Zion, the south-eastern part, or

A Place of Belonging

city of King David. Inevitably it has had a violent and chequered history, much like the Jewish people themselves. Understand Jerusalem and you have a key to understanding much of middle eastern politics to this day.

In the symbolic ordering of things, Jerusalem is a world leader. All the three major Abrahamic faiths – Judaism, Christianity, and Islam – lay a major claim to its magic. Yet the oldest of these can be traced directly to the founder, the golden king, David. The Jewish sense of entitlement is centred on the holy city. That is why we have poetry like Psalm 122:

> I was glad when they said to me, 'Let us go to the house of the Lord!' And now our feet are standing within your gates, O Jerusalem.
> Jerusalem—built as a city that is bound firmly together.
> To it the tribes go up, the tribes of the Lord, as was decreed for Israel, to give thanks to the name of the Lord.
> For there the thrones for judgment were set up, the thrones of the house of David.
> Pray for the peace of Jerusalem: 'May they prosper who love you.
> Peace be within your walls, and security within your towers. For the sake of my relatives and friends I will say, 'Peace be within you.'
> For the sake of the house of the Lord our God, I will seek your good.
>
> (Ps. 122:1-9)

INHABITING THE CITY WALL

The city walls and towers of Jerusalem protect people but also their place of worship, namely the Temple where the tribes go up to 'give thanks' and to find God. The double identity as a home and also as a place where you might meet God explains why the city enjoys such status.

Destruction and a miracle re-build

What a disaster then to realise that Jerusalem was in fact conquered and destroyed. And then re-built – and that all this happened more than once.

The most famous of all the builders of its city walls was a man called Nehemiah. Firstly, we need to start with the back story. In 598 BCE King Nebuchadnezzar invaded the city of Jerusalem. Within 12 years he had conquered the occupants, destroyed all they held dear and taken them into exile to Babylon by 587 BCE. When they were permitted to return, thanks to the good offices of the Persian emperor Cyrus, who defeated the Babylonians at their own game, a Jewish leader emerged. Nehemiah galvanised the returning Jews into a building project that meant the entire city walls of Jerusalem were restored in a mere 52 days. The year was 539 BCE.

The value of his account of this astonishing rebuilding programme is that he details all the gates in the city walls: the Valley Gate, the Dung Gate, the Fountain Gate, the King's Pool, the Sheep Gate, the Fish Gate, the Old Gate, the East Gate, the Water Gate, the Horse Gate, the Ephraim Gate – all are itemised and they provide a picture of life in ancient Jerusalem. Trade and commerce flourished; the gates became a place of meeting and exchange. Above all they remind us how porous a concept such a city wall can be. The dung collectors – bin men or refuse collectors – in modern parlance – the farmers with their sheep and horses, the fishermen with their fresh catch: all were drawn to the big city. Life prospered and hummed because the wall had holes in it. These openings meant that life could be breathed into it and that prosperity could return.

The Wisdom

These stories demonstrate how a city wall can be interpreted as a barrier, a means of exclusion; as a gateway, or place of exchange; and, intriguingly, as in the story of Rahab, as a membrane, a place of interchange which went on to become a place of escape.

The walls we build serve similar purposes. They do much the same kind of thing. First, there are the personal city walls with which we protect our own interests and aspirations. You do not have to be a psychologist to know how important these walls are. For a start, they teach us what and who we are and, more importantly, who we are not. At their best they prevent us from trying to escape into unreal versions of ourselves. We talk about having good boundaries and that means a well-developed sense of self. Only when these boundaries are secure can we learn to become selfless, for only the person with a well-developed sense of self can avoid being self-referring and selfish.

If this is true for individuals, how much more important is it for families, interest groups and even nations. No wonder enormous amounts of time and money are invested in establishing and protecting corporate identity. Group identity and national identity matter. What becomes toxic is nationalism when an over-inflated corporate ego takes over and people think that, collectively, they can do no wrong. No wonder mass movements can be so terrifying, when the crowd takes over and a kind of shared selfishness kicks in.

City walls as membranes, as places of exchange, and ultimately of love

The corrective – in the case both of individuals and of nations – is also laid out in these ancient Bible stories. Nehemiah was right: what matters are the chinks in our armour, the gates in the city walls. These are the places where we can seek out renewal and let go of our preconceptions. These represent possibilities for exchange and enrichment; these become the ways in which we learn to love.

What other demons lurk around our city walls? Arguably the greatest of these is the sense of entitlement. And nothing is more toxic than when this sense is accompanied by divine sanction. When people claim that God or Jesus or Allah is on their side, there is no gainsaying them. Even in a secular age, there are contemporary idols which are used to bolster the egos of both individuals and groups. Various lobbies adopt a moral high ground – they group around politics, around gender, even around health. And the casualties are self-evident: education; tolerance; freedom of speech; even the right to be misguided and downright wrong.

So where does escape lie? Rahab offers us an answer: be slow to take sides, inform yourself about your enemies, do not write them off. Use that red thread, signal your readiness to listen and to learn. And who knows? Your action could make you the ancestor of kings.

A Place of Belonging

We pray to the God of all protection.
We pray for the grace to be strong, to be alert, to be knowing, to be wise.
Open our hearts and minds; teach us to discern.
Show us the difference between right and wrong, and how to be unafraid.
This Lent, help us to belong to you.
Amen.

Action

- On a scale of 0-10, how is your self-esteem? On a scale of 0-10, how selfish are you?

- Where do you feel you most belong? Are you happy with your lot?

- Can you write a psalm or a hymn in praise of your home, your family and your values?

- What are your idols? How do you show your devotion to them?

- How well-defended are you? And how loving? This Lent are there any resolutions you can make that will both consolidate your sense of self and help you to become more selfless? Why not write them down?

Chapter 5
Inside the Whale – Lessons of the Deep

Introduction
In old money, it used to have a host of names: 'the slough of despond', 'feeling blue': the overwhelming sense of sadness and meaninglessness that can overtake you even when you are pretending to be cheerful. Essentially a state of mind, depression can feel like a physical condition or even – at its most extreme – it gets incarnated as a 'black dog', an animal that takes over our lives.

The Bible even has a location for it: an exact place, where an animal did indeed take over. The life of Jonah has one of its most upbeat characters go to this place of desolation in an imaginary tale. A mixture of fantasy and gung-ho adventure story, the Book of Jonah employs magical realism to cloak its deep psychological message – and above all, a hefty sprinkling of humour as the plot unfolds.

The Story
There are a series of players in this drama, and it is cast in a tight religious world that needs to be unpacked for the true meaning to emerge. There are two principal players:

there is Jonah, our hero. There is God: friend or foe? We are not certain. There are onlookers who take sides – both for and against Jonah – and for and against his God. Our narrator sets up different scenarios as his main characters move from land to sea and back again.

Our male lead, the prophet Jonah, is Mr Normal. The main thing we know about him is that he does not remotely want to be used by God for a role in the divine masterplan. His is a case of an unwanted vocation. In Act 1 of this 5-act drama, the two principal characters are well matched, and God opens proceedings by issuing a challenge. And when he is given a mission, Jonah does a runner: he bolts off in the opposite direction and chooses the most faraway destination he can think of. Anything to get away from what he thinks he is being asked to do.

Jonah's vocation

As he saw it, God had given him a task: to go to the Assyrian city of Nineveh, the largest city in the known world and to warn the people there that they were going to be destroyed if they did not mend their ways. In reality, Nineveh did indeed have a chequered history because invading Medes, Persians, Chaldeans and a host of others raided, occupied and deserted it by turns. Every up was followed by a down which gave it mythic status. Its present-day location is Mosul, on the eastern bank of the river Tigris in Iraq, a couple of archaeological tells marking the spot. Not surprising then that Nineveh has a starring role as a doomed city, right from the get-go.

So much for the 'where', the attempt the author made to locate his tale in an actual place. What about the 'when'? Scholars are reluctant to offer an exact date

Inside the Whale – Lessons of the Deep

for the book that tells Jonah's story. They assume it was written after the Jewish people returned from exile in Babylon in 538 BCE. But a reference in the Second Book of Kings (2 Kings 14:25) locates the prophet himself in the reign of Jeroboam II, namely 786-746 BCE. A case of the speculative in pursuit of the factual.

This allusion to an external source does its best to make Jonah sound like a real person. It gives him a backstory, telling us the name of his father: Amittai, and also the village in Galilee he came from: Gath-hepher. Neither piece of information is any way conclusive, nor even helpful. It simply tells us that Jonah, if there ever was such a person, came from a village about five miles north of Nazareth.

Jonah's response

So much for the facts, which turn out to be skimpy. What matters is the story: an account of someone who really does not want to do what he thinks is being asked of him. Jonah's response when God calls him is to leg it. We are told his intention was to 'flee from the presence of the Lord', to get as far away from the divine call as is humanly possible. There is nothing pious or devout about this man. He is not sold to us as a particularly holy type. He heads straight down to the seaport of Joppa – present-day Jaffa – and finds a ship which is bound for the edge of the known world, namely the opposite end of the Mediterranean Sea. There is nowhere more distant than the destination he chooses: Tarshish. A city in North Africa. Miles away – both from Joppa and from Nineveh.

Things go badly wrong for him. In Act 2, as the ship sets sail, God 'hurled a great wind upon the sea and there was a mighty tempest' (Jonah 1:4). The sailors take action: they throw their cargo overboard to lighten the ship's load, and start praying to their several gods, a medley of pagan and Greek deities. Their behaviour is totally professional. What about Jonah? What does he do? God's prophet, we are told, had 'gone down into the inner part of the ship and had lain down, and was fast asleep'. Not only is his body in flight mode, but his spirit is too. The contrast with the mariners is startling – as is the captain's reaction when he comes down to confront him.

'Get up', he tells him. And 'Get praying'. For the sailors, the dilemma is a simple one: they decide to find out 'on whose account this calamity has come upon us. They cast lots, and the lot falls on Jonah. 'Then they say to him, "Tell us why this calamity has come upon us. What is your occupation? Where do you come from? What is your country? And of what people are you." "I am a Hebrew", he replied. "I worship the Lord, the God of heaven, who made the sea and the dry land." Then the men were even more afraid, and said to him, "What is this that you have done?"'(Jonah 1:7-10).

The judgement

Their dilemma is presented in religious language. They are the devout – and innocent – victims of a situation created by Jonah and for which he must take responsibility. The language and the storyline may be simple, but the dynamic is not. As the pagan sailors see it, Jonah has pitted himself against his God. He is judged by standards he has, as it were, chosen for himself. He is responsible for his own undoing – and anyone can see that. You do not have to be a devout Hebrew to spot disobedience. Like the chorus in a Greek

Inside the Whale – Lessons of the Deep

drama, the sailors stand in judgement over Jonah, our hero, and they ask him a simple question: 'What shall we do to you, that the sea may quiet down for us?' (Jonah 1:11).

Their interests are more important than Jonah's, yet they bother to consult him. Not only are their lives in spectacular danger, but their financial security too is tied up in the viability of their boat. It represents their livelihood. And yet when he suggests they throw him overboard as they had done with their cargo, their initial reaction is to spare his life, to row harder and then they turn to prayer. The interesting thing – so far as this story goes – is that this time they pray directly to Jonah's God. Whereas their previous prayers had been directed to their own various gods, they now call on the Hebrew God, 'Please, O Lord, we pray, do not let us perish on account of this man's life. Do not make us guilty of innocent blood; for you, O Lord, have done as it pleased you.' (Jonah 1:14). Jonah, the reluctant missionary, has made a bunch of converts.

The outcome

The result is instantaneous because the sea suddenly stops raging. And Jonah's God triumphs. We are told 'the men feared the Lord even more, and they offered a sacrifice to the Lord and made vows' (Jonah 1:16). What they promised we do not know. All we can be certain of is the contrast deliberately set up between the mariners and the reluctant prophet. The pagan sailors know how to behave; the man of God does not. Our author is enjoying himself and digging a deep hole for his protagonist.

Only it is more than a hole. It is an immense fish who suddenly appears in the becalmed waters and swallows Jonah, lock, stock, and barrel.

A Place of Belonging

When Jonah wakes up to his situation and looks around him, all he can see is the interior belly of his new home. For three days and three nights he languishes there. No reference to food or drink. Just the overpowering fishy smell. The squidgy organs. The endless pink wallpaper. The directionless eddy and flow as fry and small fish float past him in the whale's stomach. The sound – worse than the hum of any submarine – of churning and belching. The bubbles, at which he gasps for air. His salvation has come packaged in a form that exceeds his worst nightmares. Act 3 has begun. Our author enjoys the irony and cracks on with his tale.

Inside the whale's belly

What does the whale's belly represent? Can this really be salvation? Certainly, it is carrying Jonah away from what went before. Namely potential shipwreck. Is he being punished? A tempting supposition because he was running away from his calling. Or is it a place of despair? The storyline is mischievous – because it admits of each of these interpretations.

Turn the focus onto Jonah and see if the three days in the belly of the whale can be interpreted from his perspective. He has been swallowed by a huge fish, several times his size and now he is experiencing enforced containment. He is stuck inside something utterly repellent, and yet it is saving him from the churning sea. He feels despair and yet he is safe. This is how his depression is configured.

The key words here are 'enforced containment'. Up until this point, Jonah has led an un-boundaried life, free – or so he thinks – to go where he will. When he felt like it, he ran away to Joppa; when he felt like it, he took a ship to Tarshish; and then, when he did not at all feel like it, he was swallowed up by a giant sea creature, a mega fish or whale. When he lost his freedom, he entered upon the slough of despond. He harrowed his own hell. A harrow is an especially vicious farm implement, designed to rake over soil that has been ploughed to ensure it is broken into small pieces, ready to be used again. To harrow hell is to make sense of the experience of death and judgement.

The harrowing of hell

If you are a fan of art history, you will know exactly what this looks like. New Testament accounts of the death and resurrection of Jesus all tell us that, when he was buried, he spent three days in the tomb. They make no attempt to explain what happened, but storytellers and myth makers cannot leave the time he spent there unaccounted for. They tell elaborate tales of how he went down to hell and visited the dead. More than that, he set about releasing them from bondage and led a fantastic procession up to heaven with the patriarchs, prophets and saints of earlier times in a long trailing line behind him. They become a tableau of the blessed. A holy conga line.

In the case of Jesus, the Christian Creed tells us his visit to the depths was redemptive. He went there to set people free; and on day three of his own imprisonment in the tomb, he burst out from it. As the Apostles' Creed has it, 'he was crucified, died and buried, he descended into hell; on the third day he rose again from the dead'. This descent into hell or harrowing is signalled here as a precept of faith and yet the words can trip off the tongue of most believers without any consideration of what they might possibly mean.

A Place of Belonging

Artists such as Fra Angelico and Albrecht Dürer have left us with awesome depictions of the actual harrowing, and it was a favourite topic for English Mystery Plays. Nor was it by chance that Dante chose to have his pilgrim visit Virgil in the First Circle of Hell in his great poem, the Divine Comedy. Going back in time means meeting up with all the characters who populated it. There is something rudimentary and deeply alarming about the level of exposure envisaged in these scenes. If hell represents your past, your whole history, if it is portrayed as a massive judgement bearing down on you, how frightening to be exposed to it in its entirety, albeit in your imagination? Is that what Jonah experienced in the belly of the whale? His life unravelled before his very eyes, and he could not escape from the re-telling of it. He could see where he had taken the wrong decisions, and that these had led inexorably to his present state. In the event, this horrific experience would prove to be his salvation. Down in the whale's belly he remembered his close encounter with death, 'The waters closed in over me; the deep surrounded me; weeds were wrapped around my head at the roots of the mountains. I went down to the land whose bars closed upon me forever' (Jonah 2:5-6).

He needed to go down before he could go up. He needed to be exposed to his own mortality. Only then could he say the transformative words, 'What I have vowed I will pay. Deliverance belongs to the Lord!' (Jonah 2:9).

The next verse gives an instantaneous result: 'Then the Lord spoke to the fish, and it spewed Jonah out upon the dry land' (Jonah 2:10). Our author is resolute. The Lord is the chief player in this story, and he is in charge. One word from him and the whale throws up her prey. She parts with what had promised to be a delicious meal.

Inside the Whale – Lessons of the Deep

Life back on shore

We might have hoped that Jonah would be a changed character after his near-death experience. The whale's belly was, after all, supposed to offer transformation, to deepen his sense of vocation, to renew his faith. It had offered him a raft of insights into his own mortality, had linked him to his past by appearing to stall any sense of a future. In a dramatic way, it had situated him in the now, in the absolute present, from which there was no escape.

But in this story Jonah emerges from the whale's belly with his flawed personality intact. Nevertheless, he did what he was supposed to do; he went to Nineveh and this required quite an effort, as the city turned out to be huge. It took him three days to walk across it and wherever he went, the outcome was the same. To his intense fury and rage, the people did exactly as he asked: they repented of their sins and turned to the Lord. Worse than that, the king of Nineveh proclaimed a fast and even had the animals take part in it, a nice comic twist on the part of our narrator.

In Act 4 of the drama, every living creature put on sackcloth and ashes, and they all repented of their evil ways. We are invited to visualise dogs, donkeys and chickens all on bended knee, their tails drooping, their eyes damp with contrition. The result was instantaneous: 'When God saw what they did, how they turned from their evil ways, God changed his mind about the calamity that he had said he would bring upon them; and he did not do it' (Jonah 3:10).

The fate of Nineveh – and Jonah's reaction

Jonah was outraged. How could this entire community take his message so seriously? How dare they repent? He

A Place of Belonging

fumed with anger, as our narrator tells us, 'This was very displeasing to Jonah, and he became angry. He prayed to the Lord and said, 'O Lord! Is not this what I said while I was still in my own country? That is why I fled to Tarshish at the beginning; for I knew that you are a gracious God and merciful, slow to anger, and abounding in steadfast love, and ready to relent from punishing. And now, O Lord, please take my life from me, for it is better for me to die than to live' (Jonah 4:2-3).

Emotionally speaking he headed straight back to the whale's belly. He tried out a strategy that could have resulted in his death, namely he went out of the city and tried to hide himself away. He even built himself a little shelter, an enclosure, a booth. But maddeningly God would not leave him alone. A bush sprouted to provide Jonah with shade which, we are told, 'made him happy' (Jonah 4:6). Then, catastrophically, God appointed a worm to eat the bush and an east wind to blow sultry air at him. Naturally Jonah vented his rage. And equally naturally, given the author's intent, God had the last word.

We are told that Jonah took up cudgels and yelled 'It is better for me to die than to live'. Our narrator lays out the psychodrama: the kind of happiness Jonah experienced when he built his little shelter was essentially transitory. It could not last because it was all about himself. Suddenly he was being exposed to a brand-new idea: that the fate of other people matters too. The great work in which Jonah had been engaged, namely the conversion of Nineveh, had brought salvation to a whole people.

> God said to Jonah, 'Is it right for you to be angry about the bush?' And he said, 'Yes, angry enough to die.' Then the Lord said, 'You are concerned about the bush, for which you did not labour and which you did not grow; it came into being in a night and perished in a night. And should I not be concerned about Nineveh, that great city, in which there are more than a hundred and twenty thousand persons who do not know their right hand from their left, and also many animals?'
>
> (Jonah 4:8-11)

And there, abruptly, with the advent of Act 5, the curtain goes down and the story ends. Jonah, our little drowned man of a hero had – unwittingly – shared in the work of God. He had helped bring about the salvation of a whole people. Unlike the ignorant people of the great city of Nineveh, he had been invited to look at their reality with the gaze of God. To feel deep compassion and to offer the chance of repentance and ultimately of redemption. Despite himself, his message, his call to conversion and a new way of living had worked.

The Wisdom

In this curious tale, different locations stand out: the cabin in the boat where Jonah slept and the whale's belly; the vast city of Nineveh and the little booth. All are shelters and mirror images of each other. The belly conceals Jonah by hiding him away in an inner world and the booth shelters him in the outer world. What he is offered in either space is time for reflection, for self-discovery and ideally transformation. If only it were that easy.

A Place of Belonging

What can be learnt in the belly of the whale?

Taken figuratively, the belly symbolises a return to the womb, to a place of re-birth. In the symbolic ordering of things, human beings naturally create womb-like experiences. We seek out spas; we go on retreat or away-days; we seek out situations that re-energise or re-create us.

The ingredients are fairly constant: there has to be a physical element to what we do. Very often this involves water and light. The spa experience is therapeutic because it takes us back to our watery origins. How helpful, how healthy to feel exposed to the sound, the feel of warm water and to sense its energy and power. How helpful to feel cleansed by our exposure to something that once carried all of us in our own mother's bellies. The primal element presses all around us and proves to be life-enhancing.

And, of course there is jeopardy: the experience of birth and the experience of re-birth take us to a new place: we harrow our own hells. We rake over our past. The image of a harrow is so powerful because it has spikes and these break up the surface of the presentation we have so carefully cultivated. On retreat or away days, we experience withdrawal and that is frightening, largely because we are exposed to ourselves and that usually means to our own back story as well. How to heal our own history? As Jonah discovered in the belly of the whale, we need to face our own mortality. The interplay of the English words tomb and womb is not accidental.

What happens next?

That insight can drive us in two different directions: either we can experience such exposure as a punishment or else, more positively, as a release. The punishment bit is easy to understand because very often our past seems to stand in judgement over us. We remember all our mistakes; everything we did – or got – wrong. We hear the echoes of our own stupidity. We recall the people who disapproved of us. The situations we screwed up. The relationships that failed. In the lonely environment of the whale's belly, everything looms large, and it is so hard to inhabit the moment, to live in the present when the past threatens to overwhelm us.

What about the other outcome? The feeling of release? The transformation promised by the whale's belly is the gift promised by the saints lined up in those medieval pictures of the harrowing of hell. Salvation. What would salvation be like for you? For most of us salvation means release, freedom, renewal. In a word, the experience of re-birth.

When Jonah is spewed up on the shore, he is presented as a man with a mission. You could be forgiven for thinking he has accepted his vocation and now he puts it into action. He sets off for Nineveh. But this transformation is not a wonder cure and, reassuringly, as we have seen, he remains as intractable as ever. That is why he is furious when his mission succeeds, and the people turn to God and are forgiven. True conversion takes time.

A medley of emotions

There is only one point in this entire story when we are told that Jonah is happy, and that is when he is sitting in the booth he has built – the mirror image of the whale's belly – and enjoying the shade provided by the little plant God has provided for him. Indeed, we are told that he is 'very happy'. In this moment of calm, Jonah experiences the one emotion that can liberate him.

A Place of Belonging

Tragically he cannot really enjoy it, because God once again intervenes by destroying the beanstalk that had given him so much pleasure. And all to offer him a far deeper understanding: his own distress at its destruction was as nothing compared with the concern God would have felt at the destruction of the great city of Nineveh. Put like that, of course the scale of Jonah's private disaster is relativised. It simply does not matter. Yet the reader could be forgiven for hating God at this point. Flexing an emotional muscle in Jonah's psyche feels like point scoring.

We cannot help but take sides. And most of us feel for Jonah and put ourselves in his shoes and experience his distress. Does this matter? Maybe it serves as a sharp reminder that there is one emotion that really is a sign of redemption: happiness. When Jonah's happiness is snatched away from him, we recognise real trauma.

When we speak nowadays about mental health, we are inclined to forget that sometimes we find it hard to say we are unhappy. It sounds somehow naïve, so we opt for the more dramatic language of health and sickness. For that reason, we might ask what if the greatest form of re-birth − for us personally, in the first instance − were simply the ability to say: 'I am really happy'? This would mean valuing the simple experience of being alive, of emerging from whatever whale has swallowed us up.

How about reading the moment when Jonah feels genuine happiness as the real moment of his liberation? The authentic Jonah relaxes into the experience, feels good about himself and his circumstances. This would explain why he is now ready to face up to the true meaning of his story. The little allegory of the destruction of his gourd plant, compared with the possible destruction of Nineveh lays bare a truth that he can only now hear for the first time: we can be saved from our own experience of disaster. When he thinks about the fate of other people instead of concentrating on his own, there is a switch in his entire mindset. Jonah can enjoy the gift of life in its fulness. Which is why the story ends. And so very abruptly.

What about God in the Jonah story?

No analysis of the Jonah story can leave its portrait of God — the divine protagonist — without comment. One thing that Jonah has a real gift for is projections. His God is almost as mercurial as he is himself. The God who pursues him is as relentless in his chase as is Jonah in his attempt to escape. None of us wants to make such a powerful enemy as Jonah's God. None of us expects the extreme experience he had to undergo to experience salvation. No wonder Jonah wanted to get away from this monster God.

Our author offers no explanations, no interpretation. He lets the facts stand and speak for themselves. As the story unravels, its true meaning emerges. Is this why the Jonah saga has a unique hold on the imagination — and all because of the unenviable destiny that is represented by the whale's belly? None of us wants to face death by drowning, but equally there is danger in re-birth too. The horns of this particular dilemma are laid out here in a saga of self-discovery that is prepared to examine the journey into the depths, as well as any scaling of a height. An account of self-discovery that is also a saga of

A Place of Belonging

God discovery: the God Jonah most hated and feared was the one he had created in his own image and likeness. Liberation, when it came, proved to be such a simple thing: the human spirit craves life – not as a personal possession but as a gift to be shared. And Jonah, for the first time ever, felt really, really happy.

> *We pray to the God of all our births and re-births.*
> *Come to us in all the circumstances of our lives.*
> *Free us from fear, especially our fear of the future.*
> *Free us from fear, especially our fear of you.*
> *Shelter and protect us; show us how to be happy.*
> *This Lent, help us to belong to you.*
> *Amen.*

Action

- See if you can find a copy of Francis Thompson's poem 'The Hound of Heaven', written in 1890. You should find it online at http://www.houndofheaven.com/poem Thompson was destined to be a doctor but wanted to be a poet. He fell on hard times in London, became an opium addict and died aged 47.

- Can you recall an experience of re-birth? Or, more importantly, an occasion when your eyes were properly opened to the plight of someone other than yourself?

Inside the Whale – Lessons of the Deep

- Why would you flee from God? Is the God you are fleeing from real, or an invention you have concocted for yourself?

- Think about the parallels between the shelter of the whale's belly and the season of Lent. Can you list them?

Chapter 6
Beside the Well

Introduction

How good are you at sharing? At thinking about other people and their needs? Do you try to avoid appeals on your time and good will? Sometimes we are generous without even thinking about it. At other times fear kicks in: is this situation going to demand more of me than I can give? Is this needy person going to turn out to be a total pain, asking more of me than I am prepared to give? And in any case, is there enough to go round?

Sharing is about stuff, evidently, but it is also about ideas. Who formed yours? Do you ever make a conscious effort to refresh your thinking? To explore other ways of looking at things? Where do you get your news from? If you enjoy radio and television, are you a news 24 junkie or do you prefer tuning in to music? Do you use social media for your news gathering? How do you feel about people who disagree with you or hold the opposite point of view? Do you enjoy sharing your ideas? Where do you do this with most abandon?

Self-evidently nowadays the Internet has become an amazing source for us: a wellspring of information and potential. All that is best and all that is worst about human nature pours out of it. Importantly, we do have enough experience to discover whether what we find there contributes to building up or destroying human community, to promoting learning and true scholarship or to spreading lies. To filter its contents, we need to test it, obviously, to lean down into its depths and sample it; to apply the same strategies as we would to check out any other medium. Discernment is all.

For wisdom and insight, turn to ancient stories that have a distinctive setting, namely that astonishing place human beings discovered when they first began to dig holes in the ground and found that water bubbled out of them. When they realised the miracle could be harnessed: when they created wells.

So much happens beside a well. Where water flows, so does human interaction. People congregate, they chat, they barter, they fall in and out of love. Because it offers a moment of relaxation, they devise plans, dream dreams, and find inspiration, or produce fresh ideas. Even a watercooler can attract a gathering and become a place where opinions get shared, strategies decided, friendships formed. The shared experience of thirst draws people together. Add to that all the other attributes of water – and this convergence seems totally natural.

The experience of water

Is this because as much as 60 per cent of the human body is made up of water and we naturally seek it out? We are drawn to this vital element because we already enjoy such a close relationship with it. More than that we share this experience with every other living organism. Water washes through all of animal and plant life; it even hydrates the planet, the oceans that surround us, the air we breathe, the life force that pulses through us.

Speaking practically, we need it to drink, self-evidently, but we also need water to wash, to cook. A desert people, like the early Hebrews whose stories are told in the Bible, were more aware of this than we need to be. Access to water became synonymous with survival and, in an age of faith, an abundance of water became a sign of God's mercy and love.

The Story

Where to begin? There are innumerable well stories in the Bible: stories that describe the experience of looking for water, and also of looking for everything that water symbolises.

Discovering an oasis

To start with the literal search, we can engage with the escaped slaves who are on the run from Egypt. On the west side of the Sinai Peninsula, the wandering Israelites, under their leader Moses, found a resting place. When they made a miraculous escape across the Red Sea, they thought they had a short march ahead of them. In the event it would take them a full generation, namely the symbolic forty years, to reach what they called the promised land. As they trudged along under a burning sun, they began to suffer from thirst and then they came to a place called Elim. It sounds like the perfect oasis: 'Then they came to Elim, where there were twelve springs of water and seventy palm trees; and they camped there by the water' (Ex. 15:27).

Imagine the sensation for people who had experienced exclusion. After the extremities of slavery and of their panicky escape, they were able to flop down among the palm trees and enjoy the shade they were offered. The combination of water and shelter makes for a haven. Humans and animals alike can collapse in the shade and find instant refreshment. No hassle, no negotiation: just the sweet experience of gulping the miracle of water that pours out of the secret source below their feet. And then a picnic of dates under the shelter of the palm trees.

In such a context sharing becomes natural. The water and shade provided in an oasis are not personal possessions. They are there for everyone. The number 70 used to describe the palm trees is as much a symbol of limitless abundance as the water itself.

Small wonder that water takes on powerful allegorical meanings and that it becomes a metaphor. Life-giving and life-affirming, it stirs the imagination, and we reach out to touch the well-springs it represents. And it is because of this trajectory from somewhere deep to somewhere available that it becomes inspirational to contemplate the experience of water springing out of the ground. Looking for a deeper meaning, this experience becomes a metaphor for our deepest longings, for the certainty that true wisdom can spring out of nowhere or even somewhere seemingly implausible, such as deep inside us.

The well in Samaria

In the next story, recorded in the Gospel of John, Jesus is also on his way somewhere. In chapter 4 of the text, we learn that he has been down by the river Jordan in Judea and now is returning to his home territory, namely Galilee. Freshly baptised by his wild and wonderful cousin, John, he comes to a well and, like the runaway slaves at Elim, he is thirsty. So far, so good. But there is a complication. This well is in Samaria, the former ancient Kingdom of Israel and what is identified these days as the West Bank of the River Jordan. Samaritans and Jews did not get on, even though both were subject to Roman rule. At this period in history, all their territory was occupied and yet this failed to create a shared bond. Their past was too toxic for that.

When he was making his way back north, Jesus had, of necessity, to pass through this hostile territory. We are told that when he came to a settlement called Sychar, his disciples went off to find food and he sat down beside a well. The noontime sun beat down and he had no bucket to get at the water. He needed someone to share their access to the life-giving spring that supplied this particular well. At that moment a woman appeared and as she prepared to draw water, Jesus spoke to her.

At this point the sky should have fallen in on both of them, because both were breaking convention. Jesus should not have spoken to a lone woman, and she should not have spoken to a Jew. What happened next moves the story on from the literal to a stack of other levels. The metaphorical, the allegorical, the spiritual. All are quarried as Jesus and the woman begin to spar. John takes up the story:

> The Samaritan woman said to him, 'How is it that you, a Jew, ask a drink of me, a woman of Samaria?' (Jews do not share things in common with Samaritans.) Jesus answered her, 'If you knew the gift of God, and who it is that is saying to you, 'Give me a drink', you would have asked him, and he would have

given you living water.' The woman said to him, 'Sir, you have no bucket, and the well is deep. Where do you get that living water? Are you greater than our ancestor Jacob, who gave us the well, and with his sons and his flocks drank from it?' Jesus said to her, 'Everyone who drinks of this water will be thirsty again, but those who drink of the water that I will give them will never be thirsty. The water that I will give will become in them a spring of water gushing up to eternal life.' The woman said to him, 'Sir, give me this water, so that I may never be thirsty or have to keep coming here to draw water.'

(John 4:9-15)

The Samaritan woman resolutely hangs on to her line of argument. She is talking about water, about the stuff in front of her which she is busy drawing into her bucket. This Jewish man, who appears to think himself greater than any of their shared ancestors, holds out an improbable hope. He seems to be promising a magical kind of water that will satisfy her thirst for ever. Can you imagine? She can – and gazes into a future that promises no more trips to the well, no more unwieldy buckets, no more heavy lifting. No wonder she is keen; no wonder she wants to get hold of this water and does not hesitate to ask for it.

There is a further twist to this story where the symbolism of the well takes on a new urgency. Jesus wants her to drill down, to experience something more important than her immediate thirst – or even his own. As he sees it, their conversation must go deeper, so he sets her a trap.

Beside the Well

Contested identities

> Jesus said to her, 'Go, call your husband, and come back'. The woman answered him, I have no husband'. Jesus said to her, 'You are right in saying, "I have no husband"; for you have had five husbands, and the one you have now is not your husband. What you have said is true!'
>
> (John 4:16–18)

She is smart enough to realise what is going on and comes back at him with what she reckons is an unassailable argument. She is not going to be fobbed off with slurs about her sexual history or be treated as a woman of loose morals. Rather her Samaritan hackles are raised, and she tackles him about the religious conflict that separates her people from his. If he is so knowledgeable, what about the status of their spiritual practices?

> The woman said to him, 'Sir, I see that you are a prophet. Our ancestors worshiped on this mountain, but you say that the place where people must worship is in Jerusalem'. Jesus said to her, 'Woman, believe me, the hour is coming when you will worship the Father neither on this mountain nor in Jerusalem. You worship what you do not know; we worship what we know, for salvation is from the Jews. But the hour is coming, and is now here, when the true worshipers will worship the Father in spirit and truth, for the Father seeks such as these to worship him. God is spirit, and those who worship him must worship in spirit and truth'. The woman said to him, 'I know that Messiah is coming' (who

is called Christ). 'When he comes, he will proclaim all things to us'.

(John 4:19-25)

The wider picture

At this point it is worth pressing a pause button to situate this conversation within the wider context of John's Gospel. The most carefully crafted of all the four gospels, John's has an underlying pulse: it is driven along by a sequence of six significant stories. Each tells the reader about a miracle – from the gift of water turned into wine at a wedding feast to the raising of a good friend from the dead. These miracles are called signs because they point beyond themselves and throw significant light on who Jesus was, as recorded in John's Gospel.

The story of Jesus' encounter with the Samaritan woman at the well comes after the wedding at Cana, a small town in west Galilee and before the healing of an official's son at Capernaum to the north of the Sea or Lake of Galilee. Jesus is trying things out, reaching out beyond the known circle of friends who gather for a marriage feast. He has disciples, followers who think the world of him, he has received the endorsement of his calling at his baptism, and now he is beginning the work to which he believes himself to be called. When he gets back home to Galilee he will heal the son of an official in Capernaum. The unnamed official has only to ask and the miracle occurs, thereby confirming his identity as healer. At the well in Samaria, he tries out another skill: can he teach? Can he find the right idiom, the right degree of challenge, the right illustration to bring his message home to a single individual? By testing the waters, he is discovering the scope of his vocation and ministry.

BESIDE THE WELL

The story takes over

Hearing his explanation, the woman is able to recognise what he is saying. She knows about the promise of salvation wrapped up in that term Messiah and then, amazingly, we learn that Jesus said to her, 'I am he, the one who is speaking to you'.

> Just then his disciples came. They were astonished that he was speaking with a woman, but no one said, 'What do you want?' or, 'Why are you speaking with her?' Then the woman left her water jar and went back to the city. She said to the people, come and see a man who told me everything I have ever done! He cannot be the Messiah, can he?'
>
> (John 4:27-29)

The rest is history. His teaching has worked: people come out from the little town because of what she tells them, they too believe in his message and after a couple of days, he moves on. There is a sting in the tail: of course, the townspeople then say to the woman that they believed because they got what Jesus was saying to them directly. Their conversion had nothing to do with her or the testimony she had given. Yet again a woman is left stranded, with her account of the meeting dismissed as irrelevant. She re-assumed her status as one of the marginalised, someone whose experience did not really count.

Indeed, her conversation at the well would be completely forgotten had Jesus not thought it important. He ensured that the details were remembered. After all, the encounter had supplied him with a metaphor. He spoke freely to her of 'the water that springs up into eternal life' and this figure of speech was set to be an image of what he wanted to bring to life in her – and in all of those who would receive his teaching. On this occasion – as so often when Jesus is interrogated by a woman – the learning goes two ways: he gains clarity about his identity and role; she finds her own truth. For both of them, the discovery was revealed beside the well. Both had drunk from the bucket lowered into the same source and to each of them it delivered the truth that came with the gift of its waters.

The well of Jacob

A final detail: the place where Jesus and the Samaritan woman met was not just any old watering hole: it was called the 'Well of Jacob' recalling happier times when the patriarch Abraham's grandson Jacob had settled down there to enjoy his old age.

Abraham's son was Isaac. When he was 37, his father Abraham set about finding a bride for him. The account is the closest the Hebrew Scriptures come to a truly romantic love story and unsurprisingly, it features a well. The elderly Abraham sends for his oldest and most trusted servant and commissions him under oath to go and find a young potential bride for his son from among his own kindred.

> Then the servant took ten of his master's camels and departed, taking all kinds of choice gifts from his master; and he set out and went to Aram-naharaim, to the city of Nahor. He made the camels kneel down outside the city by the well of water; it was toward evening, the time when women go out to draw water. And he said, 'O Lord, God of my master

> Abraham, please grant me success today and show steadfast love to my master Abraham. I am standing here by the spring of water, and the daughters of the townspeople are coming out to draw water. Let the girl to whom I shall say, "Please offer your jar that I may drink", and who shall say, "Drink, and I will water your camels" —let her be the one whom you have appointed for your servant Isaac. By this I shall know that you have shown steadfast love to my master.'
>
> (Gen. 24:10-14)

All goes according to plan, for out comes an enchanting young woman who shares the abundant water from the well with him and then draws more for the ten camels to drink. Her name is Rebekah and she turns out to be a cousin of her future husband. And of course when they meet, they fall in love, so he takes her into his mother's tent and the dynasty goes marching on.

Beside a well, anything can happen – and it does.

The Wisdom

These stories from the Bible, even when randomly selected – as is the case here – are underpinned by a common set of values. They assume there is a lot of water, even if most of it is hidden underground. They also assume that the water is there for everyone. All that is needed is a well, a bucket, a cup and the gift can be shared. This water is genuinely intended for everyone and access to its abundance is meant to be for us all. In that way it can realise its symbolic meaning, which is about shared thirst, shared humanity, and sharing our deepest values. The biblical wells demonstrate how people discovered their thirst, their identity and their ability to love.

Living with Wells

When it comes to making these connections, I have an advantage: I live in a city called Wells, in Somerset. The water that pours out of the ground in the springs that well up in the garden of the Bishop's Palace comes from the Mendip Hills. These hills are porous because they are formed of limestone. You can see the life cycle of a raindrop manifesting before your very eyes as the water in the moat around the Palace changes colour according to what is happening in the fields up on Mendip. Most of this water is drawn off to join a local river; the rest is channelled to run in gutters down the length of the High Street, a gift to the citizens from a former bishop.

The well water that bubbles out of the ground to feed the river brought prosperity to this little English city. It powered its mills during the medieval period: grain became bread; sheep's wool was washed, spun, and turned into capital; even silk was produced from the force the tumbling water generated to run the merchants' looms. Water meant prosperity and the presence of the wells secured an endless supply of this.

Much earlier, the original Roman settlement of the city was sited where the wells produced their water. Unsurprisingly the invaders built a shrine there to honour their gods and, equally unsurprisingly, this was where the Saxon king, Ine, laid the foundations for a place of Christian worship in the year 704. The Romans loved water – and they loved lead, which they mined just up the road in the Mendip Hills. Some 20 miles away they built a shrine at a site called Aquae Sulis – the waters of Sulis – where boiling hot water poured out of the ground at temperatures exceeding 95 degrees centigrade. Sulis was a Celtic goddess, and the Romans chose to use the name Minerva for her, Minerva being their goddess of wisdom and healing. A golden mask of Minerva can still be seen in the Roman Baths Museum in modern-day Bath. Water became a multiplier, bringing prosperity certainly, but also healing.

This is a story that could be replicated all over the world: water brings life, settlement, prosperity, a sense of gratitude, and then healing. Unsurprisingly wells and springs become places of worship or shrines.

Building a shrine

The association of water with healing explains why the Celtic people who preceded the Romans chose to build shrines where they did. And this in turn explains why so many English churches, especially in the south of the country are sited near wells and streams and rivers. So often they replaced so-called pagan shrines, places where people already reckoned they had experienced an encounter with the divine.

An experience of healing is also seen as integral to this meeting. After all, what kind of a useless god would produce water that has no healing properties? People looked for a double miracle. The moment water came seeping out of the ground; the moment it could be brought up to the surface by digging a well; the moment it could be channelled and brought to work in people's homes was miraculous enough. No wonder people equated its appearance with a divine revelation. When, in addition, this water had the power to cure and to heal by virtue of its mineral and chemical content, this double miracle was celebrated with rituals and festivities. Traditions such as 'well dressing' carry the memory of happier times. In Derbyshire, this tradition is associated with the end of the Black Death, the plague that decimated the countryside in 1348. Well-dressing or well-flowering continues to this day, blending superstition and practical common sense. For the miracle of water should never be taken for granted.

In our own times, we associate big brands with the production of healthy water: Buxton, Highland Spring, Perrier, Vittel, Evian, San Pellegrino. The names trip off our lips and supermarket shelves as we drink our way to salvation. The marketing of spa water is a triumph of modern consumerism – as well as a nightmare because of the environmental damage caused by the mountains of plastic bottles it has generated.

Because it comes from the sky as well as from deep underground, we understand that water is free and the village well is for everyone. The wells in the Bible provide us with imagery: they remind us to dig deep for the treasure that lies beyond everything we can actually see. This treasure is not always clearly defined: what nourishes me at a given moment may not do so for ever; what satisfies you just now may not last. We change; we grow and so do our expectations and our true selves and our deepest needs. How important then to be attentive to what we really desire and need.

A deeper meaning

The stories we attend to are powerful because they tell us about people meeting each other or discovering their own deep desires. But there is a further dimension beyond this personal search for our dreams: in the simple gesture of lowering a bucket down into the depths and offering it to a stranger, even a foreigner, they speak powerfully of the value there is in sharing.

The oasis at Elim became a place of abundance because there was water for everyone: for the people and for their animals. It secured the salvation they thought they had been promised. No conditions, no negotiations, just gift. The woman at Jacob's well would never have discovered the recognition and redemption she needed without the choice she made to give the gift of water to the man who asked her for a drink. And Rebekkah, Isaac's bride, is identified by her readiness to share water from her father's well.

In the gospel story, Jesus himself identifies as living water. The water he speaks of 'gushes up'. It is full of energy and cannot be contained. When people share water some of that energy is handed on. So too with the content of our dreams and deepest desires. When we share them, we hand on the energy and life they represent, and it too becomes 'living water'. With the gift of water comes the gift of life as the people discovered by the oasis at Elim. When you share ideas and good news, you share your dynamism, as the woman at the well discovered. When you share your life and make new relationships, you change the world, as Rebekkah discovered. Thirsting for meaning, for identity and for love, we too are invited to share our experience of discovery.

A detail: no one has to go digging in the ground in any of these biblical stories. There is no spadework involved: no one builds a well. All that is required is to be attentive and willing to explore. The deep already exists; the water is already given. Your own well is ready for you to draw from its depths. The task is to discern and decide. You are the moral agent, the one who lowers the bucket.

The imagery is powerful – and so is the sheer impetus of finding power underground and propelling it and being propelled by it. Deep within ourselves we have the power and creativity to drive forwards and to seek the freedom and healing represented by the gift of water freely given at a well. Once we discover that wisdom, we will also find that the instinct it to share can be transformational.

We pray to God who gives us wisdom along with water.
Teach us to dig deep.
Share your abundant gifts with us.
Teach us to treasure your wisdom and to share it.
Spring up to life in us.
This Lent, help us to belong to you.
Amen.

Action

- Turn on a tap; fill a glass with water and drink it. Try to visualise the long journey the water has been on to get to your mouth, your tongue, your gullet, and the long, complicated journey it is now embarked upon to nourish your body. Imagine it mingling with your cells and becoming a part of you.

- The psalm writer put his longing for God into words that rely on the power of water for their impact.

  As a deer longs for flowing streams, so my soul longs for you, O God.
  My soul thirsts for God, for the living God. When shall I come and behold the face of God?
  My tears have been my food day and night, while people say to me continually, 'Where is your God?'
  Why are you cast down, O my soul, and why are you disquieted within me?
  Hope in God; for I shall again praise him, my help and my God.
  My soul is cast down within me; therefore I remember you from the land of Jordan and of Hermon, from Mount Mizar.
  Deep calls to deep at the thunder of your cataracts;
  all your waves and your billows have gone over me.
  (Ps. 42:1-3, 5-7)

- Find a way to experience the healing gift that comes with water. It may be that you feel inspired to share something, to be spontaneous and give something valuable or precious to someone else. Some gesture that demonstrates your realisation that there is enough to go round. Fill your bucket and give someone a drink.

- Take a look at the websites of aid agencies that specialise in the provision of clean water globally: https://www.wateraid.org/uk/ or https://toilettwinning.org/ for instance. The three disciplines of Lent are prayer, fasting and almsgiving. What better alms to give than the gift of water?

- Once again, the assumption is that the impetus to share makes for a better world than the impetus to hoard. In present-day political life it is often counter-cultural to put the needs of other people before our own. Do you think that privilege brings responsibility or is it simply an opportunity to get richer quicker?

Chapter 7
The Fiery Furnace – A Double Whammy

Introduction

When were you last in extreme danger? What is the worst experience you have had to endure? What is your greatest fear? Most of us, at some time in our lives, will have to pass through a fiery furnace. How well resourced are you? What could help? Who could help?

What about other people? What is the ultimate disaster that can happen to someone else? What about losing your home? This is the ultimate displacement, losing your place, your space in the world. This, as we know all too well, is the fate of a host of people in our times. Whole populations are made homeless by war, by economic or climate devastation. And we watch this happen because the images of their misery get transferred into our homes by satellite and onto our TV screens. We find ourselves watching other people as they walk through fire. Troublingly now, the natural reaction when we wonder how we can help is increasingly accompanied by a sense of utter powerlessness. Then disinterest, a lack of compassion and a sense of irrelevance can trickle in. Eventually we even become numb. Mission fatigue becomes our normal.

A Place of Belonging

The Story

There is a bizarre one-off story told in the Bible about three young men who are consigned to the flames of a blazing furnace by a megalomaniacal ruler. This weird story has a curiously contemporary ring.

The King of the Universe

The king in question is called Nebuchadnezzar. Cue a biographical note: to situate him in time – he ruled from 605-562 BCE, and in place – Babylon. He had a lot of names: King of Assyria, King of Sumer and Akkad and – best of all – King of the Universe. Clearly he was a man whose modesty knew no bounds. Among his achievements: the creation of an empire and a series of building projects, including the Hanging Gardens of Babylon, one of the Seven Wonders of the Ancient World. He swept all before him, including the city of Jerusalem which he sacked in 586 BCE, an event known as the Babylonian Captivity.

It was when they were place-less and homeless that the Israelites began to identify as Jewish. During their exile, when they were displaced, the community began to develop a distinct culture and identity. Their self-knowledge and religious practice were formed in a crucible as extreme as any fiery furnace. It sounds like a cliché, but the reality is that they developed their sense of nationhood at this time of exile and through all this hardship. They were fashioned in the fire of adversity.

Four young men

When they came to write down the tale of what they went through, they chose to tell the story of young men who became symbols for what the whole nation went

The Fiery Furnace – A Double Whammy

through. These were major players and also survivors, a word that has come to have huge resonances for a whole community of people.

Back at the time of the Babylonian captivity, and most fortunately for the exiles, they had a hero at hand. A young man called Daniel emerged as a leader. He had been transported away from Jerusalem with three friends: Hananiah, Mishael and Azariah. In the biblical Book of Daniel we learn that because they were young and bright and good-looking, they were brought to the Chaldean imperial court in Babylon to be trained as fledgling diplomats. Their training was rigorous because they were to be transformed into an elite. According to the story they went through a series of trials, all designed to test their suitability and also to check how important it was to them to remain true to their Jewish identity. Could they be relied on? Would they be malleable? According to our story, they stuck to their principles, refusing food and drink that went against the dietary rules they wanted to keep, because they considered what they were being offered to be defiled. An impasse beckoned until, providentially, Nebuchadnezzar began to be troubled by a series of dreams and Daniel turned out to have a gift for interpreting them.

The King of the Universe had a nightmare: he saw a giant statue made of four different metals: gold, silver, bronze and iron. This statue could not resist as a mysterious hand emerged that started to stone it to destruction. He set a task for his magicians and diviners: they were to tell him what he dreamt and then offer an explanation of the hallucination he had had.

No one could help. After all, the task was impossible.

A Place of Belonging

How do you interpret a dream when you do not know what it was about? At that point the Chaldean king abandoned his diviners and turned to the young Jewish outsider.

As interpreted by Daniel, the dream became a revelation about the future of the empire. There were to be four identifiable kingdoms, represented by the four different metals and then came the hideous interpretation: ultimately Babylon was doomed. Rather surprisingly the king rewarded Daniel by promoting him to a role at court. He was flattered by an interpretation that set his own time up in office as a golden reign. He also elevated the young Jewish companions. They were to be officers of state and dispatched to work in the empire. Daniel remained at the centre where he could be called on for further dream work.

The giant idol

Nebuchadnezzar meanwhile devised a scheme to cement his own sovereignty: he had an enormous golden statue built. Then he organised a party, inviting 'the satraps, the prefects, and the governors, the counsellors, the treasurers, the justices, the magistrates, and all the officials of the provinces to assemble and come to the dedication of the statue' (Daniel 2:2-3). Only when they were all assembled was his true intention revealed. The megalomaniac had a cunning plan.

> The Book of Daniel takes up the story:
> When they were standing before the statue that Nebuchadnezzar had set up, the herald proclaimed aloud, 'You are commanded, O peoples, nations, and languages, that when you hear the sound of

The Fiery Furnace – A Double Whammy

> the horn, pipe, lyre, trigon, harp, drum, and entire musical ensemble, you are to fall down and worship the golden statue that King Nebuchadnezzar has set up. Whoever does not fall down and worship shall immediately be thrown into a furnace of blazing fire.'
> (Dan. 2:4-6)

The fate of Daniel and his young friends was sealed because of course they would not go against their principles; the king had misunderstood. He had chosen to forget that these particular young men could not worship an idol. The blaze of sound from the musical instruments sealed their fate. Enforcers from the king's palace reported back to him and Shadrach, Meshach, and Abednego – to give them their Babylonian names – were arrested and brought before the king. In this new guise, cemented by these names into their roles as aspirant princelings and no doubt terrified to find themselves under suspicion, the three young men were wheeled into the sovereign's presence.

Trial by fire
The story takes over.

> Nebuchadnezzar said to them, 'Is it true, O Shadrach, Meshach, and Abednego, that you do not serve my gods and you do not worship the golden statue that I have set up? Now if you are ready when you hear the sound of the horn, pipe, lyre, trigon, harp, drum, and entire musical ensemble to fall down and worship the statue that I have made, well and good. But if you do not worship, you shall immediately be thrown into a furnace of blazing fire, and who is the god that will

deliver you out of my hands?' Shadrach, Meshach, and Abednego answered the king, 'O Nebuchadnezzar, we have no need to present a defense to you in this matter. If our God whom we serve is able to deliver us from the furnace of blazing fire and out of your hand, O king, let him deliver us. But if not, be it known to you, O king, that we will not serve your gods and we will not worship the golden statue that you have set up.'

Then Nebuchadnezzar was so filled with rage against Shadrach, Meshach, and Abednego that his face was distorted. He ordered the furnace heated up seven times more than was customary and ordered some of the strongest guards in his army to bind Shadrach, Meshach, and Abednego and to throw them into the furnace of blazing fire. So the men were bound, still wearing their tunics, their trousers, their hats, and their other garments, and they were thrown into the furnace of blazing fire. Because the king's command was urgent and the furnace was so overheated, the raging flames killed the men who lifted Shadrach, Meshach, and Abednego.

(Dan. 3:14–23)

This epic visual description is merciless. We can see the king's face reflected back to us a curious shade of orange, lit up by the flames and his own rage. Of course, the guards who throw the young men into the flames are expendable, but the detail of their death is a horrible reminder that slaughter generates slaughter and where death becomes commonplace, it creates its own casualties.

But this was not the end for our young men.

The Fiery Furnace – A Double Whammy

The three men, Shadrach, Meshach, and Abednego, fell down, bound, into the furnace of blazing fire. Then King Nebuchadnezzar was astonished and rose up quickly. He said to his counsellors, 'Was it not three men that we threw bound into the fire?' They answered the king, 'True, O king.' He replied, 'But I see four men unbound, walking in the middle of the fire, and they are not hurt; and the fourth has the appearance of a god.' Nebuchadnezzar then approached the door of the furnace of blazing fire and said, 'Shadrach, Meshach, and Abednego, servants of the Most High God, come out! Come here!' So Shadrach, Meshach, and Abednego came out from the fire. And the satraps, the prefects, the governors, and the king's counsellors gathered together and saw that the fire had not had any power over the bodies of those men; the hair of their heads was not singed, their tunics were not harmed, and not even the smell of fire came from them.

Nebuchadnezzar said, 'Blessed be the God of Shadrach, Meshach, and Abednego, who has sent his angel and delivered his servants who trusted in him. They disobeyed the king's command and yielded up their bodies rather than serve and worship any god except their own God. Therefore I make a decree: Any people, nation, or language that utters blasphemy against the God of Shadrach, Meshach, and Abednego shall be torn limb from limb, and their houses laid in ruins; for there is no other god who is able to deliver in this way.' Then the king promoted Shadrach, Meshach, and Abednego in the province of Babylon.

(Dan. 3:23-30)

A Place of Belonging

An amazing volte-face as the king literally takes up the cause of the God venerated by the three young men. He has witnessed a miracle — not only did the fire not destroy them, but also they were joined in the flames. They did not go to their fate alone. Moreover, Nebuchadnezzar was the only one to see the fourth figure. To Shadrach, Meshach, and Abednego, their saviour was invisible.

The Wisdom
Fire and the promise it brings

How are we to understand such an ancient and unpredictable story? What help does it offer us today? The image of all-consuming flames is one we can hardly bear to contemplate: we know how ambivalent fire can be. Of all the four elements — earth, air, fire, and water — fire seems to be the most primitive, with the greatest ability to become destructive. We use it for domestic purposes, to cook our food and heat our homes. We associate it with warmth and comfort. But when it gets out of control, it can reduce a promising meal to cinders or, much more devastatingly, it can ravage a tower block in central London, destroying a community, their homes and livelihoods. We are right to be terrified of it.

None of us will be able to forget the image of Grenfell Tower burning like a flaming torch in June 2017 and sending 72 of the people who lived there to their untimely deaths. In reality fire holds total terror for us because it gets out of hand so desperately quickly. It consumes everything it meets. When it comes to symbolic meaning, fire has no competitors: it is the ultimate enemy.

In the case of warfare, it has an especially brutal role. It becomes a third party, attacking both sides with equal

The Fiery Furnace – A Double Whammy

violence, the weapon of both. Ever since the discovery of gunpowder, its use has spiralled as its internal violence take hold. This violence is especially visible when bush or wildfires become commonplace, when nature itself combusts and begins to devour itself. A wildfire on earth looks so like the images of raging planets far out in the universe where every form of energy is somehow unleashed in a molten frenzy.

Yet even its powerful, destructive nature can be harnessed and made to serve a purpose. Fire is used in alchemy, in transformation. It changes the very nature of what it touches. Fire is used in industry, to generate energy. Fire is used in medicine, to cauterise. That is why a fiery furnace is also a crucible, a place where new ideas and things come into being.

The experience all the Jerusalem exiles underwent was one of displacement: trial by the fire of being dispossessed and transported into a new land. Then, for Daniel's three young companions, came the double whammy, the actual physical fire which threatened to destroy every trace of them. Fire destroys skin and flesh and, at its most extreme, even bone. Only memory remains intact and that too can be insubstantial because it gets eroded by time.

Seared on the Jewish people's consciousness, this experience of exile foreshadowed the many historical traumas through which they would have to pass down the centuries as they became a persecuted and ghettoised community. Pogrom has followed pogrom culminating in the attempted annihilation of the whole people in World War II's Europe. Small wonder that the use of furnaces in the great twentieth-century slaughter of the Jewish holocaust is also recalled with such horror.

A Place of Belonging

Nowadays we inhabit a world where huge swathes of humanity are on the move because they too have been displaced by war or famine or economic happenstance. The awful symmetry caused by war in the Middle East creates fresh casualties in which the holocaust experience seems to be replicated. The word genocide resumes its place in common parlance. The story of the young men in the fiery furnace takes on a horrible relevance.

Is there a pattern in the Book of Daniel that might speak to our experience nowadays as we struggle to find a way forward in a world where more refugees are being created, and nationalism rears its ugly head?

The refugee experience

We bandy about words such as integration and inculturation. Long Latinate words that fail to describe the experience of having to fit in and understand 'the system'. This is what happens when you have made the long journey away from the known and the familiar place and way of life you called home. Imagine what it must feel like when the entire onus for being accepted sits on your shoulders, when you become the refugee who has to make all the running, literally?

Put it the other way round and think about the experience of the host community too. These long words fail to meet their lived experience when people who live in a named street have new neighbours who speak a foreign language and cook up food that smells different. The stereotypes are all too familiar and so easy to parody. Curry is fine in a curry house, but not when the scent of turmeric, cinnamon and cumin fills a lift shaft in a block of flats and does not shift. The smell of roasting lamb and

The Fiery Furnace – A Double Whammy

baking flatbreads is strange. Throw on a handful of oregano and it becomes alien.

Foreign clothes are fine when worn by picturesque people in their own setting. Our holiday photos show amazing sights and of course, local colour in the form of the old man with the prayer beads or the burkha-wearing woman with her adorable baby show that we really have been there. But what happens when they pop up back home, in places where we feel we belong and where we want to live?

Then there is language. Certain accents are acceptable because the native community finds them sexy or even intelligible thanks to half-remembered language lessons. Others appear to be raucous or threatening. They can even sound downright funny. The feelings we have towards the sounds we hear transfers effortlessly across to the people who make these sounds. The stereotypes verge on the racist.

Then there are people's names. Foreign names are so hard to say, let alone to spell. Is that why Hananiah, Mishael and Azariah became Shadrach, Meshach, and Abednego? The suggestion is that their new Chaldean names make them acceptable in the alien world represented by Babylon? And what does that mean?

There is a sense in which becoming 'more like us' or 'accepting our standards and values' is a form of purification. Part one of the double whammy of moving continents. But equally there is a commitment for the host community. How to accommodate the incomers and to ensure they have the opportunity to flourish as the young men were supposed to do.

How to find a balance? The transformation offered

by fire should surely work both ways. In the cauldron represented by the fiery furnace, purification means learning acceptance and recognising the value of the 'otherness' of other people, however painful this might be. This works both ways. Both the conquering Chaldeans and the incoming Jews were offered transformation when the initial effects of conquest began to kick in.

Integration

Shadrach, Meshach, and Abednego were what we would nowadays call 'high status': bright, attractive young men, potential high-flyers. Doctors, lawyers, politicians in the making. No wonder they seized the educational and social advantages they were offered in Babylon. But even they had their sticking points. What mattered to them cut to the very heart of their identity: they were, by any account, the wrong religion. And on religious matters, they would not compromise. On one level the Book of Daniel offers a running commentary on the issues raised by multiculturalism when it is founded in religious difference. How very pertinent.

The young men had to learn how to operate in the new life they had embarked on. What should go? Their original names for instance, as they sounded too foreign? What should stay? Their fundamental beliefs, meaning worship of the monotheistic or one God; and their observances such as special dietary restrictions. These gave them a distinctive identity and made them identifiable. By hanging on to their religious beliefs they believed they were hanging on to their very being.

In an age of uncertainty, where religious belief seems out of date, something that belongs to yesterday, any sense

The Fiery Furnace – A Double Whammy

of the sacred is under threat. In a climate of active hostility to religion, how easy it becomes to dismiss the religious practices and belief systems of incomers. Their worship is scorned as primitive; their mosques, gurdwaras and synagogues as quaint. Religion is blamed for everything that is wrong with the world because religious people have waged war on each other to such dramatic effect, claiming that God is on their side and wreaking havoc in the name of their beliefs. Religious conflict turns out to be more toxic than any other precisely because it is wrapped up in identity.

In a climate of benign indifference, the consequences are even more devastating: no one actually cares what you believe – and that is daunting for people who invest in their belief system, again precisely because it is so closely identified with their identity.

There are so many reasons why we find it hard to understand the conviction of the three young men who went into the fiery furnace as martyrs for their religious faith. Yet go they did and let us follow them there. Why on earth would we do that?

Because we want to be transformed.

Transformation

The fiery furnace promises a unique experience. The forging of identity. For Shadrach, Meshach, and Abednego what they experienced when the flames burned round them there was a real discovery. They found they were not alone. The God they had worshipped from afar came down into the fire and took the hit with them. Their reaction: an amazing song of praise as they understood what was going on. Their faith was vindicated and so were they personally.

A Place of Belonging

The identity they had defended by praying to their Hebrew God, by observing certain rituals and avoiding certain foods suddenly stopped being something they secured by doing things. It became something they were.

What happened next? In the midst of the fire, they began to sing a hymn of praise and thanksgiving to the God who saved them. This song has been adopted by the Christian Churches as a core element in its playlist of worship, literally an elemental way of integrating belief and practice and hopes and fears. Known as the *Benedicite,* it holds a central place in Christian liturgy as a lyrical outpouring of praise, even in the midst of adversity.

An irony though: this song is not printed in Protestant Bibles. It belongs to a body of literature called 'The Apocrypha' that gets published alongside the main Bible in Catholic versions. But the Song of the Three Young Men is not secret or suspect, rather it was beautifully translated for inclusion in the Book of Common Prayer in 1662. A song of triumph, a song of praise, it sings blessings to the God who saved and who continues to save.

From the heart of the fiery furnace, the young men sang:

> O all ye Works of the Lord, bless ye the Lord:
>   praise him, and magnify him for ever.
> O ye Angels of the Lord, bless ye the Lord:
>   praise him, and magnify him for ever.
> O ye Heavens, bless ye the Lord:
>   praise him, and magnify him for ever.
> O ye Waters that be above the Firmament, bless ye the Lord: praise him, and magnify him for ever.
> O all ye Powers of the Lord, bless ye the Lord :

The Fiery Furnace – A Double Whammy

> praise him, and magnify him for ever.
> O ye Sun and Moon, bless ye the Lord:
>   praise him, and magnify him for ever.
> O ye Stars of Heaven, bless ye the Lord:
>   praise him, and magnify him for ever.
> O ye Showers and Dew, bless ye the Lord:
>   praise him, and magnify him for ever.
> O ye Winds of God, bless ye the Lord:
>   praise him, and magnify him for ever.
> O ye Fire and Heat, bless ye the Lord:
>   praise him, and magnify him for ever.

In this way they even acknowledged that God made the fire that enveloped them, associating fire and heat – along with the whole of the rest of nature – with the great blessing that they were experiencing. The God who came into the fire and suffered alongside them was the very God who had made the fire in the first place.

Narrative technique

Only they did not sing this at all, or certainly not at the time the events took place, if take place they did. This story took some time to transition from oral or spoken literature to a written text. Its oral origins are easy to detect: you can imagine the storyteller with his use of frequent repetition – those amazing musical instruments for a start, listed as they are a couple of times – the recurring use of the boys' names as a mental hook to keep the storyline moving on, the little vignettes provided by dream sequences. There is no reference to Daniel himself in this particular account and this is taken to indicate that it formed a separate narrative that got inserted into the book that bears his name.

A Place of Belonging

When did this happen? When was the book of Daniel written down? The events it describes date from the sixth century BCE but most commentators attribute the written text to an unknown scribe writing in the second century BCE, four hundred or so years later. It is a complicated book, written in Hebrew, Greek and Aramaic, indicating that the writer was juggling his diverse sources. Only the ultimate meaning is clear: God looks after the chosen people, whatever the odds because human kingdoms come and go. The reign of God goes on beyond that of an overambitious megalomaniac, beyond all the titles and honours he heaps upon himself and the gardens and towers he builds. Beyond the legislation he enacts to cripple the enterprise of others. Beyond the wars he promotes, beyond the overwhelming scope of his naked ambition.

This message is intended to be comforting and the image of the young men in the fiery furnace holds the key to understanding it. Their story becomes an emblem, a symbol of the fact that – according to the belief system of our author – God comes down among the flames.

What this means in Christian thinking

This insight becomes fact in the Christian understanding of what was going on when Jesus is born. He is sent by the Father and his triple ministry of teaching, healing and preaching is sanctioned by the Spirit. Matthew's Gospel summarises his mission in a sentence: 'Jesus went throughout Galilee, teaching in their synagogues and proclaiming the good news of the kingdom and curing every disease and every sickness among the people' (Matthew 4:23).

The Fiery Furnace – A Double Whammy

The whole thrust of the Christian gospel places him among the flames of the furnace we call the human condition. He is born, lives and dies directly in the firing line of those flames because his work is about embracing the human condition in its fulness. And being human means courting disaster and displacement and breakdown and tragedy. There is no avoiding it. The flames stand for our lived experience, not simply for the idea that we can survive disaster but also for the fact that we can and do live through it as well.

The Book of Daniel has a sobering message: disaster happens. The story of the three young men contains a promise: there is life within and beyond disaster. The presence of a fourth figure among the flames holds out hope. The Christian Gospel gives that hope a name and a face. Hope becomes a person in the living, transforming presence of Jesus among us, even in the heart of the fire. This understanding has generated all that is best about the Christian way of life. If you like, it has fuelled the fire in the belly of all the most godly and benign of the saints; equally, it has condemned those who have failed to grasp this essential truth to what have been called the fires of hell.

We pray to the God of strength and glory,
true ruler of the universe.
Reveal your power to us in all the circumstances of our lives –
Where we triumph and where we fail.
Be with us when we need your comfort and protection
And may we, in turn, bring the warmth of your love
to others in their hour of need.
This Lent, help us to belong to you.
Amen.

A Place of Belonging

Action

- Light something: a candle, a match, a gas ring. Do you have a sense that you are releasing danger or power? Feel the heat. Do you experience fear, or hope, or something else?

- Read this account of a theophany – an event where God as revealed to an individual.

  Moses was keeping the flock of his father-in-law Jethro, the priest of Midian; he led his flock beyond the wilderness, and came to Horeb, the mountain of God. There the angel of the Lord appeared to him in a flame of fire out of a bush; he looked, and the bush was blazing, yet it was not consumed. Then Moses said, 'I must turn aside and look at this great sight, and see why the bush is not burned up.' When the Lord saw that he had turned aside to see, God called to him out of the bush, 'Moses, Moses!' And he said, 'Here I am.' Then he said, 'Come no closer! Remove the sandals from your feet, for the place on which you are standing is holy ground.' He said further, 'I am the God of your father, the God of Abraham, the God of Isaac, and the God of Jacob.' And Moses hid his face, for he was afraid to look at God.

  (Ex. 3:1-6)

- Have you ever thought you were standing on holy ground?

The Fiery Furnace – A Double Whammy

- Luke's Gospel has a telling line: Jesus said, 'I came to bring fire to the earth, and how I wish it were already kindled!' (Luke 12:49). How comfortable do you feel reading that?

- Recall an experience where you too have passed through a fiery furnace. Did you feel alone? Who helped you survive? Could you be the fourth figure for a friend?

- Could you use these words with any integrity: 'O ye Fire and Heat, bless ye the Lord: praise him, and magnify him for ever'?

- We live in a world where every land could be a promised land and every people a chosen people. What is your land? Who are your people? Think big: 'Enlarge the place of thy tent, and let them stretch forth the curtains of thine habitations: spare not, lengthen thy cords, and strengthen thy stakes' (Isaiah 54:2).

CHAPTER 8
ALL AT SEA

Introduction

How confused are you? Are you afraid of mental fragility? Are you fearful of losing your way through the myriad tasks and interactions even the simplest of days holds out to you? Are you ever embarrassed by your inability to recall a face or a name or a word? Do you lose things? Or do you lose any sense of time? Do you lose your way?

Confusion like this is so widespread that we cast about for explanations. Is it something in our food, in our drinking water? What is causing the phenomenal rise in illnesses such as dementia, with UK statistics set to rise to 1.1 million sufferers by 2030? Why do most of us know someone with Alzheimer's?

In addition, confusion and disorder in the inner world so often mirror chaos in the outer world. This outer disorder too is evident as never before. It is present on our screens and in our ears as the fate of nations is relayed by 24-hour news bulletins. It is especially evident when the news is of collapsing financial markets or political mayhem. It is evident in the ways that climate change and pollution manifest in our world. We are becoming too rich, too poor, too hot, too cold, too wet, too dry. Not only do we seek for explanations, but also we devise strategies, ways of coping. At moments like this, as we become aware of how vulnerable we are. We seek the security and salvation offered by safe places. We want an end to our anxiety, to both outer and inner distress.

The Story

In short, we want an ark of salvation. Only we would never call it that. Consider the advantages though: what a blessing to be able to cast off the burden of everyday concerns and cares, to leave behind everything that tethers us to the here and now. What bliss to choose a couple of nice animal companions and sail off into the sunset.

Only of course it would not be like that and, as we shall discover, that is not what an ark is for.

The alternatives seem so clear: fight or flight. It seems that we can either escape from all that troubles us or we can engage with it. Escape towards an idyllic land of total freedom or engage with the human project and its sheer messiness. True salvation, for most of us, lies in grappling with our problems, rather than withdrawing from them. And to do this, we do indeed need an ark, conceived now not as a means of running away or escaping, but as a way of facing all that troubles us. Like a sturdy boat, it can offer us a way to ride the storm. If there is an ark, it is intended for us to survive the high seas, not to sail into the sunset. We are too closely bound into the web of relationships and concerns that tie us into our own particular reality to get away that easily. To our cost, we know we cannot vanish or abandon the fray.

This means thinking about the true function of an ark of salvation. Is it a means of escape or does it offer us an opportunity to be involved in what is happening to us, day by day but, miraculously, from a place of safety? By reflecting on one of most ancient and powerful myths that human history has preserved for us, we have a template for survival. The flood story from the Book of Genesis is designed to help us do just that.

The Noahs

Enter Noah, stage left. Here was a man who was deeply alarmed when he received the divine command to build a boat, to fashion his own ark of salvation. The story is one of the best known of the early myths that are retained in the Bible. There was this man: Noah. There was his wife, Mrs Noah. And the children, Shem, Ham and Japhet, with their unnamed wives. There were the animals, lots of them, all neatly paired as they marched up the gangplank into the boat that Noah had built. It was massive: 450 foot long by 75 foot wide and 45 foot high, and through its windows the assembled company watched in horror as cascades of water began to pour out of the sky. By way of comparison, imagine ten London buses end-to-end, by two buses high. A monstrosity of a ship and of course, completely unseaworthy. A timely reminder that we are in the land of myth.

According to the story, it rained and rained and rained. Rain tipped down in torrents, without let up, unremittingly, for forty days and forty nights. And eventually the boat parked up on a mountain side in modern-day eastern Turkey, at a site called Mount Ararat. Here Noah released a bird to see if it would come back with good news. The raven soared off up into the soggy sky and did not return. It had better things to do. Noah sent a dove off on the same mission. We are told that it could not find any dry land and returned to the safety of the ark.

A Place of Belonging

When the dove was next sent out on a scouting mission, the news was better: it returned with a freshly plucked olive leaf in its mouth. Noah waited another seven days for the waters to subside, sent the bird out again and, when it did not return, let down the gangplank. Noah, Mrs Noah, the three sons with their wives and all the living things who had been on board the ark with them marched forth and set about repopulating the earth.

Why?

Why had there been a flood? Why were the Noahs preserved? Why were the animals not condemned to die in a watery grave? What about everyone else?

The account given in the Book of Genesis is one of many flood stories that circulated freely in ancient mythology. The area between the rivers Tigris and Euphrates, known as the 'Fertile Crescent' gave rise to at least nine different flood stories. The one that most resembles the Noah story is recounted in the Epic of Gilgamesh, an ancient Mesopotamian epic poem about the origin of the known world. But there is a startling difference. The gods who send the flood in the old Babylonian myth have no reason for what they are doing. They flood the earth. People die. Some live on to tell the tale and life goes on. In the case of the Genesis flood, the emphasis is quite different. Noah's God deliberately sends the flood, with the intention of destroying human life. All right, Noah and his family and the animals are saved, but there is a reason for this.

Noah's is a moral universe. His God stands in judgement over human wrongdoing and the flood is sent because the earth and its people are corrupt. Its waters will destroy everything and thereby restore the state which the Bible calls chaos. This is how the world was deemed to be before the creation stories at the beginning of the Book of Genesis. It was, if you like, the pre-creation state and now, from that chaos, a new creation will emerge, led by Noah who had been judged blameless and who is to be spared. The flood becomes a means of punishing human sinfulness. When the dove returns to the stricken ark, perched on the side of Mount Ararat, the fresh green olive leaf represents forgiveness as well as peace. It is God, we are told, who breathed new life back into the earth by making a wind blow so that the waters would subside. The threat of chaos was lifted when creation was newly restored.

What happens next?

No wonder the first thing Noah does when he makes his way out of the ark is to build an altar and make sacrifices to his God. An indication of the antiquity of this primitive story comes from a detail given in the text. We are told that 'the Lord smelled the pleasing odour of the burnt offering' and said in his heart,

> 'I will never again curse the ground because of humankind, for the inclination of the human heart is evil from youth; nor will I ever again destroy every living creature as I have done. As long as the earth endures, seedtime and harvest, cold and heat, summer and winter, day and night, shall not cease.'
>
> (Gen. 8:20-22)

This God has nostrils and likes barbequed food.

A Place of Belonging

Our author recognises that 'the inclination of the human heart' may be unpredictable, but nature (represented here by the ground); and its stability (represented by the ebb and flow of the seasons) is sacrosanct. Just as the earth bore the heavy burden and destruction of the flood, so too will the earth experience redemption. And as a sign that this is the case, God says, 'I have set my bow in the clouds, and it shall be a sign of the covenant between me and the earth' (Gen. 9:13). The promise is a concrete one and it is to be manifest in a rainbow, a natural phenomenon that can be seen by everyone. The sky fills with coloured light and nature is vindicated.

The most powerful language used in this account of the flood story sets up the supreme relationship between God and the earth. And then, almost as an afterthought come promises of a covenant between God and 'every living creature of all flesh', animals and humans.

> 'When the bow is in the clouds, I will see it and remember the everlasting covenant between God and every living creature of all flesh that is on the earth.' God said to Noah, 'This is the sign of the covenant that I have established between me and all flesh that is on the earth.'
>
> (Gen. 9:16-17)

The flood story places Noah and his family firmly where they belong, within nature, not apart from it and certainly not above it. Human wrongdoing is catastrophic, and its outcomes are devastating for nature, for our physical reality, for the entire universe, for the earth and 'all living flesh'. Redemption, when it comes, must be for the whole of created reality, not simply for the human beings who ruined everything in the first place. This account of catastrophe has an extraordinarily contemporary ring.

The Wisdom
Noah's ark in art and literature

Such a chastening story has proved to be a goldmine for artists. The sight of polar bears and ants solemnly marching two by two up a gangplank, closely followed by orangoutangs and butterflies provides a visual feast for painters. Musicians as well have been inspired and so we have Benjamin Britten's *Noye's Fludde* of 1958 or the Disney film *Fantasia 2000*. The theme of global destruction is mined in dystopian novels too. Most hang on to the theme established by the Noah story, that human beings are responsible for their own destruction.

The drama is intensified where the world conjured up in these stories is cast as a religious one. God becomes a player and the plot thickens as the authors engage with the inevitable psychodrama of cause and effect. They raise questions about the how and the why. In the flood story, God's role is not of a capricious ogre, bent on destruction and mindless terror. The beauty of this early story is that it holds a delicate balance: God is both the maker of mayhem and the giver of salvation. God causes the waters to rise up and flood the earth, and also breathes life back into the chaos by sending the wind that will dry the ground and restore it. The true moral agents, the people who cause the flood are the people who do wrong in the first place. If there is blame, they should indeed take the punishment as they merited it. They cannot pass the buck because they deserved what came to them.

A Place of Belonging

This is a tough message because of course – in this mythological account – innocent lives were lost. The flood story does not want to dwell on this aspect of what it portrays. But the same holds good nowadays. Even a cursory glance at our TV screens shows us the casualties of war and we can see quite clearly that no one is spared by the brutality of what happens when the tanks begin to roll. Famine too strikes everyone when an entire population is starved. A nuclear explosion has no other purpose than total annihilation. The innocent are destroyed along with the just. If anything, this fate compounds the guilt of those whose folly brings about the initial catastrophe.

What does this story mean?

The Noah story has a simple message: you cannot blame God for human caprice. All you can do is hope that you too will be able to locate an ark and that you too will avoid the consequences of human sinfulness.

Does this sound defeatist? Or like a cop out? You could argue the exact opposite: that it restores a moral compass to the human project. We cannot back out of the fray by arguing that we are powerless and that God is to blame for everything that is wrong with our world. Or that God is a simple human invention, dreamed up by primitive peoples as a kind of bogeyman to take the stick for everything that is wrong with our world. Or, worse than that, to administer the stick and beat us all up when we do wrong.

Whether you have religious faith or not, you have moral authority and that brings responsibilities that cannot be ducked. Indeed, they should be nurtured and cared for. Just as Noah had to care for his family and for the animals on the ark.

All at Sea

Taking care

Is this what is meant by joining the fray? When we accept our full humanity, we buy into a time frame. Not only do we accept that we are part of the natural world and not superior to it, but we become subject to its laws. And this means embracing the cycle of nature, with its inevitable push and pull, its instability and movement, its essential seasonality. Life and death take up their rightful place in our thinking.

When she was first diagnosed, the philosopher Gillian Rose, who died of cancer at the age of 45 in 1993, wrote memorably,

> I will stay in the fray, in the revel of ideas and risk; learning, failing, wooing, grieving, trusting, working, reposing – in this sin of language and lips.
>
> (Gillian Rose, *Love's Work*)

Joining the community formed by the ark is a way of engaging, of joining in, taking part in the 'revel of ideas and risk'. Rather than symbolising escape, this massive boat becomes a means, a vehicle rather than an obstacle to the human project.

The ark of human life sails on tempestuous waters. We cannot stay still. Like us, these raging waters come and go. The Noah story is all about movement and some movement is deeply unsettling.

Moving into old age

This is especially true of the movement we all must make into old age. This is when outer chaos and inner uncertainty seem inexorably to move together as if drawn by a magnet and we become prey to turmoil and confusion. How hard it becomes to believe in ourselves when physical pain takes over from youthful certainty; when clear sightedness gives way to bewilderment; when everything becomes an effort, and it takes double the time to achieve anything.

The trouble with old age is that it is natural and utterly normal. And yet so costly. This is because of the inherent dynamic of nature which is towards decline. The life cycle really is just that, a cycle and eventually it loses it impetus and slows down.

As human beings live for longer with improved diets and access to amazing medical care, our physical health appears to be more secure than it has ever been. But there is no guarantee that our brains can keep up. We lose brain cells at an astonishing rate and the resulting cognitive impairment spares no one. Even the healthiest of old people, those whose brains appear 'bright as buttons' suffer from memory loss.

Dealing with human fragility

How to cope? How to find an ark of salvation? The flood story suggests that companionship holds a key. The waters may rage but we are offered a way of surviving the rising tide. Never has the presence of other people been so important; never have animals assumed so prominent a role in our happiness and sense of security. We do not, we must not, travel alone.

Then there is the reaching out, the sending of messages from the security of the ark in the form of ravens and doves. In today's world much of our own messaging is electronic, and why not? Like the birds we too may inhabit the air waves, and this means ensuring that we do not create a society in which there is an information divide. There is so much debate about the harmful effects of mobile phones and tablets and the internet on young people that we sometimes forget that they can hold out a lifeline to older people.

Computers mirror human brains and can act as extensions to our own memory and understanding when our powers begin to fail. Internet word puzzles, matching up games, crosswords, jigsaws all become mental workouts. And, in turn, the zoom call, the email, the playlist and online photo album become prompts, ensuring continuity between the past and the present, the security of belonging to our own story and that of those we love. Above all, music becomes a lifeline, tying up the past to our own personal Mount Ararats, to places and events which serve to anchor our memories.

Interpreting the storm

The flood story is not the only biblical narrative to offer a water-borne slice of wisdom. One of the Bible's most lyrical poems takes up the theme with an account of an adventure on the high seas. The image of wind and waves is explored as a way of understanding human vulnerability.

Unbridled power in nature exposes us to our immense fragility. Again, what is at issue here is an examination of human motivation, of the psychology of fear. In Psalm 107 we read,

> Some went down to the sea in ships, doing business on the mighty waters;
> they saw the deeds of the Lord, his wondrous works in the deep.

A Place of Belonging

> For he commanded and raised the stormy wind,
>   which lifted up the waves of the sea.
> They mounted up to heaven, they went down to the
>   depths; their courage melted away in their
>   calamity; they reeled and staggered like drunkards,
>   and were at their wits' end.
> Then they cried to the Lord in their trouble, and he
>   brought them out from their distress;
> he made the storm be still, and the waves of the sea
>   were hushed.
> Then they were glad because they had quiet, and he
>   brought them to their desired haven.
>
> (Ps. 107:23-30)

When the storm is stilled, the promise is that there will be calm and that we will reach our own particular haven. The promise is of hush and eventual quiet. Beyond trauma lies the simple human emotion of joy as the sailors realised that they 'were glad'. Such happiness brings true release.

A sleeping saviour

No account of sheer vulnerability of humankind in the face of our own mortality would be complete without the lakeside adventure Mark gives in his gospel. This examines the relationship Jesus enjoys with the wind and the sea.

> On that day, when evening had come, he said to them, 'Let us go across to the other side.' And leaving the crowd behind, they took him with them in the boat, just as he was. Other boats were with him. A great windstorm arose, and the waves beat into the boat, so that the boat was already being

ALL AT SEA

swamped. But he was in the stern, asleep on the cushion; and they woke him up and said to him, 'Teacher, do you not care that we are perishing?' He woke up and rebuked the wind, and said to the sea, 'Peace! Be still!' Then the wind ceased, and there was a dead calm. He said to them, 'Why are you afraid? Have you still no faith?' And they were filled with great awe and said to one another, 'Who then is this, that even the wind and the sea obey him?'

(Mark 4:35-41)

The boat this time is a regular fishing boat. The companions are experienced fishermen. The lake is the familiar Sea of Galilee. No big deal. But the storm is vicious, and it comes from nowhere and their skill at sailing and rowing is no match for the unbridled forces unleashed on the disciples. Jesus himself? The great teacher and miracle worker? Well, he is asleep. Mark's narrative is almost comic in the contrast it sets between the sleeping saviour and the terrified crew. Like Jonah in the story of the whale's belly, our hero is spark out, exhausted by his day's work.

Once roused from his cushion, Jesus takes control. He rebukes the wind and orders the sea to be still. And the result is instantaneous: there was 'a dead calm'. Again, beyond trauma, there is an outcome when peace returns.

The agent this time is Jesus himself. His power over the wind and the waves is evoked as a demonstration of his divine authority. Like God in the flood story, he assumes ultimate control and the little fishing boat becomes an ark of salvation.

At this point the Christian story offers a happy ending. But does this work in reality? For most of us the conundrum remains: how do we cope with our most elemental fears? The wisdom of the Flood story reminds us that rescue is possible: we can build an ark and, thanks to the shelter it provides for us, we can survive. The people who did not survive the Flood, according to the account in Genesis, were those who had already taken themselves out of the fray by denying that they inhabited a moral universe. In their world, actions have no outcomes. They create chaos by thinking in a vacuum where there is no right or wrong.

In the post-Flood world, the newly created world to which we are carried on an ark of salvation, we come to 'our desired haven' and can receive the olive branch of peace and forgiveness. The great reveal of the Noah story is that there is an end to all that troubles and threatens to overwhelm us. Beyond the crippling anxiety we can experience as we face our own mortality lies the certainty of the ultimate ending, of death. The anxiety is completely natural and normal, but so too is the resolution. The secret is to engage – while we can, and to the best of our ability. 'Learning, failing, wooing, grieving, trusting, working, and eventually - reposing.'

We pray to the God of our salvation, our ultimate ark.
Free us harm and crippling anxiety.
Your desire is for us to be free and to be happy.
Bring joy into our lives so that we may experience your love in its fulness.
This Lent, help us to belong to you.
Amen.

All at Sea

Action

- When did you last experience genuine fear? What helped you get over it? Who was there for you?

- Who is the oldest member of your family with whom you have contact? Who is the oldest person you know? Do you have concerns about their mental frailty? What can you do to ease their situation?

- When did you last experience a storm, or see a rainbow? Did you allow yourself to experience the drama of the situation?

- In your mind assemble the cast of characters you would like to take on your own ark of salvation. Remember to choose some animals. This is not to plan an escape – but to engage with the rest of your life. A really sturdy, well-provisioned ark will enable you to survive, to sail the high seas and to face up to the reality of your circumstances.

- Holy Week is getting closer. Does that fill you with dread, or with hope?

Chapter 9
The Heavens are Telling

Introduction

When you look up, what do you see? Does it make you happy? Does it make you sad? By and large looking up beats looking down: it enlarges our field of vision, rather than constricting it. Mostly, in the United Kingdom at least, we look up to check the weather. We associate the sky with some sort of promise – of rain, of sun, of a storm or a downpour. It presents us with an instant forecast of what is to come. Somehow what is happening in the skies above our heads communicates the future to us more intensely than merely feeding back a reflection of the present. Unlike the slow-moving landscape around us, our skyscape is constantly changing; it speaks to us of potential, of what could be. And, of course, we look up in the knowledge that our planet is in perpetual motion along with the rest of the cosmos.

At night the panorama evolves and becomes immense, even when the sky is covered over. What appears to be one dimensional in daylight suddenly goes into 3D mode as the varied planets and stars take up different positions and circle over our heads. The one apparent constant, the moon assumes different shapes as it plays hide and seek with planet earth. We know the night sky has the capacity to be our friend as it helps us locate ourselves and to form a relationship with its constellations. For centuries the sky has been the ultimate navigational aid for seafarers and anyone wanting to explore the unknown. They could look up and know where they were.

This exciting sense of contiguity has been reduced in our own times. The glare of light pollution blocks out our access to the night sky. The closest most people get to the stars is through the astrology pages of their newspapers or websites where predictive powers are attributed to star signs. Or analogously where celebrities too are paraded before us, along with astonishing stories of their rise to stardom. Small wonder astrology has such a potent grip because of its supposed powers of fortune telling. It retains the connection our ancestors experienced between what they could see and what lay ahead in the unknown future. No wonder too that astronomy rejects its claims in the name of science. The study of the stars has to be objective if they are to help us find our place in the universe. Only this way does 'homecoming' become possible and can we discover where we belong.

Space as our physical context

We do not invent the sky and the solar system and the immensity of galaxies that form our physical context. They are a given. No wonder we want to know more about them. So far, we have been unable to do more than gaze and examine and explore through bigger and bigger telescopes, space travel or, in the case of the moon, to pay a cursory visit. Add what the theoretical understanding of physics and mathematical exploration have brought to the mix, and you can understand why scientists excite us with even more revelations about how space actually works.

A more recent development has seen the very rich taking to the skies. The link between celebrity and the stars appears to be validated when a rocket can be launched taking the girlfriends of the super-rich and sundry celebrities into space. And so we have a new phenomenon: space tourism, a leisure activity for wealthy nations and individuals.

Winning and losing in the realm of space

True scientific space travel brings material benefits evidently. These range from space-age valves for vascular surgery to the simple foam-pumped running shoe, via a host of inventions that enable us to live a more comfortable life on earth, rejoicing in our amazing communications systems while frying our bacon in non-stick pans.

There is also a psychological shift and this possibly is less wholesome. Rather than inspiring a sense of awe at the enormity of the cosmos, human beings seem doomed to develop an even more grotesque sense of superiority to that we already claim as an 'alpha' species. The immensity of the known and unknown – especially the unknown – has failed to teach us any kind of humility or give us a sense of proportion.

Witness a downside to the space adventure that lies just out of vision: as on planet earth, multiple space launches produce garbage or junk. We live with the knowledge that discarded satellites and the detritus of space exploration encircle the atmosphere above our heads. Metal carcasses of failed or abandoned projects collide with each other and mingle with unplotted meteors. Even where we cannot quite see the evidence, we have the horrible certainty that planet earth is surrounded by rubbish as failed or worn-out satellites join the debris we cast into outer darkness.

Out of sight, out of mind – for the moment. This is a form of colonisation that seems unable to recognise the problems it is storing up for itself. And, thinking further ahead, when human beings do go to Mars or set up outposts beneath the moon's surface, they will inevitably take human nature with them. Behaviour-wise we can expect more of the same. As the Jesuit poet Gerard Manley Hopkins wrote in his poem, 'God's Grandeur' of 1877, 'all is seared with trade; bleared, smeared with toil;/And wears man's smudge and shares man's smell.'

The bitter truth is that we will take ourselves and our problems wherever we choose to go. Human garbage generates space junk, produced by flawed human beings. This has a message for us. How come that the lessons of colonisation have yet to be understood, so that an unconscious sense of superiority and entitlement accompanies our 'conquest' of space? This surely is the ultimate hubris. We exhibited it quite unconsciously with the first thing we chose to photograph when, as a species, we first ventured into space, claiming it as an extension of our own habitat. We took 'selfies', photographing the blue planet, the beautiful marble of the earth and publishing them in every printed outlet possible as proof of our achievement. Even now they dominate the internet's presentation of space travel. You could be forgiven for thinking we go into space only to gaze – Narcissus-like – at ourselves; that the most remarkable thing we discovered in space was planet earth.

The Heavens are Telling

The cost of human elitism

Along with this hubris, as a by-product of the elitism it engenders by plonking human life, human culture, human enterprise at the top of every kind of tree, comes a merciless intolerance of anyone prepared to think differently. This becomes an inability to conceive that there might be anything or anyone superior to us. No spirit- or life-form can be superior to our own. If much of contemporary atheism is predicated on an over-valuing of our place on the planet, then inevitably there are those who anticipate that any belief in a creator God will be unable to survive the discoveries of the scientific community. Contrarywise, it is of course true that much superstition and naïve beliefs have to go when confronted with facts that dismantle a literal reading of say, the Bible.

Yet genuine belief in a God who is supreme spirit and exists independently of created reality can and must survive human attempts at interpretation. This is a cool God in both senses of the word. I am not alone in being happy to nail my colours to this kind of belief, largely because it rules out certainty and triumphalism and all the attitudes that have got the practice of formal religion such a bad name. Let God be God and not simply a projection of human inadequacy or superstition or an idol of our own making.

How we interpret the heavens – space as metaphor

Unsurprisingly, given the association we make between the sky and the future – and whatever it is that this future holds for us – and given their apparent inaccessibility, the heavens also trigger our imaginations. We look up and suddenly become visionary, excited by what we think we

A Place of Belonging

see unfolding. We see imaginary shapes in the clouds, even a man on the moon. Our spirits rise along with our raised eyes. Along with the excitement of scientific discovery, the skies offer us liberation. We begin to imagine. We dream.

Throughout history, the heavens been identified with heaven. As well as being a physical place, ancient peoples believed that this was the space where the gods had their home. In early Greek and Roman mythology and in the belief systems of the ancient near east, this assumption made total sense.

The gods had to live somewhere so it might as well be in the most unreachable place imaginable: in this case on remote mountain tops, beyond the clouds on Mount Olympus. In places where no one would ever be able to join them. Ultimate reality was predicated on the gods being 'other' and not like us, so naturally they lived 'elsewhere'. When they visited mere mortals, they did so from their vantage place on high. The fact that, when they did visit, they turned out to be as capricious and vengeful and jealous and loving and maddening as humans was what mattered. We can understand now that placing their home in the heavens, just beyond reach, demonstrates that they were psychologically very important. They served as projections, teaching humans the wisdom of learning the patterns of shared behaviours. This means understanding your mistakes as well as your triumphs.

Heavenly visitations were treasured because they were assumed to break the veil between the known and the unknown worlds. The gods could do their interfering, and then take off again, back to the Elysian fields where they belonged. The traffic all went in one direction, with them visiting us, never the other way round. Attempts to take to the sky and emulate the gods were doomed. Think of the fate of Icarus, whose beeswax wings melted when he tried to fly and went too close to the sun.

The third understanding – space as outcome

After examining heaven literally as a place, and then figuratively as an image, we can take the plunge and think of the heavens representing a destiny or even an outcome.

The Abrahamic faiths inevitably have a different understanding from the Greek one because their God, being a supreme spirit, does not need to live anywhere. The heavens become less of a place or a residence where God lives and more of a space we aspire to. Is this why we use the word allegorically: 'what a heavenly experience 'or 'heavenly day', meaning beyond the ordinary confines of loveliness. And it is why we hold out the promise of paradise as the most desirable of spaces to go after death. Paradise is a concept, an idea, not an actual place. If anything, paradise becomes the ultimate space, beyond our wildest imaginings.

Where Greek and Roman mythology focused on the underworld as the place where humans would end up when they were dead, the faith presented by the Bible looks up. Admittedly there was Sheol, where the dead descended and which is mentioned some 66 times in the early part of Bible. But above all – and especially when the Hebrew people became distinctly the Jewish people, after their return from exile – there is paradise, the home of the blessed. A concept that passed into Christianity and also into Islam. This heaven comes to have a separate, non-physical location: it becomes the preferred image for life after death: a space of ultimate comfort and meaning.

A Place of Belonging

Paradise becomes the ultimate homecoming.

Strangely, false understandings of its meaning proliferate. An obvious example might be young jihadists who are promised the thousands of virgins waiting for them in paradise them once they have perpetrated acts of violence and died for their cause. A false understanding within Islam is not the only casualty. Christianity too traded the promise of eternal life to its warring crusaders and has never hesitated to bargain for souls by using the threat of hell to intimidate the faithful. The earthly practice of excommunication supposedly mirrored this ultimate exclusion. The imagery is the same: a dramatic casting out of the offending individual along with the threat that they will never ever again belong. The psychological and emotional damage go deep and, of course, no one ever expects the Spanish Inquisition.

The Story
A story told in poetry

There are so many threads to unpick in any attempt to reclaim the true meaning of paradise. In this hinterland of metaphor and allegory, the best poetry in the Bible comes into its own. To make any kind of sense of the notion of our place on planet earth, or of the heavens as home in an afterlife, we can get a steer from a book that goes back thousands of years: the Book of Psalms.

As in the case of the Greek and Roman myths, the cosmology may be primitive, but the understanding of human nature is not. That is why these ancient texts repay exploration. They have a theological framework, certainly, but they also have a psychological and inspirational one too. They can help us look up and out and beyond ourselves with a degree of self-understanding.

The Heavens are Telling

Planet earth

The primary insight is based on a territorial one, about what belongs to whom. The psalmist is certain: 'The heavens are the Lord's heavens, but the earth he has given to human beings' (Ps. 115:16). Along with this comes a clear delineation: our author wants to make it quite clear that there are different ways to seek for meaning and purpose. Why should the nations say, 'Where is their God?' The psalmist is interested in the idea of what governs our actions and choices. A god made in the image and likeness of humankind cannot have any autonomy. Such a god would merely replicate us – over and over again. Whereas, as our writer sees it:

> Our God is in the heavens; he does whatever
>   he pleases.
> Their idols are silver and gold, the work of human
>   hands.
> They have mouths, but do not speak; eyes, but do not
>   see.
> They have ears, but do not hear; noses, but do not
>   smell.
> They have hands, but do not feel; feet, but do not
>   walk; they make no sound in their throats.
> Those who make them are like them; so are all who
>   trust in them.
>
> (Ps. 115:2-8)

If you relinquish control of your life to an outside influence that is simply a mirror image of yourself, you have no true freedom. The psalmist presents us with a God who 'does whatever he pleases'. This sounds a bit toxic until you realise that the sphere where this influence is exercised is elsewhere 'in the heavens'. Human beings are made in the image and likeness of this God, rather than the other way round. The Bible offers the understanding that human living is a serious affair, to be undertaken by adults who enjoy the same autonomy in their sphere – on earth – as God does in the heavens. We are not puppets on a string.

The 'otherness' of the heavens

Then there is the issue of heaven itself. Where is it and where is God? The Bible has a bewitching answer. It all depends on what you are looking for. In fact, it all depends on you. Psalm 15 is emphatic:

> O Lord, who may abide in your tent? Who may
>   dwell on your holy hill?
> Those who walk blamelessly, and do what is right,
>   and speak the truth from their heart;
>   who do not slander with their tongue, and do
>   no evil to their friends, nor take up a reproach
>   againsttheir neighbours;
> in whose eyes the wicked are despised, but who
>   honour those who fear the Lord; who stand by
>   their oath even to their hurt;
> who do not lend money at interest, and do not take
>   a bribe against the innocent.
> Those who do these things shall never be moved.
>
> (Ps. 15:1-5)

The tent where God dwells or the holy mountain where this sacred tent is established is not a physical place: it is a space where our attitudes and actions are assessed and found to have huge consequences. In a word they can bring us to heaven. This space, while available to everyone, can only be accessed by people who have deliberately adopted a certain way of being. Namely by those who consciously choose to live by the truth and to take other people seriously.

If anything should inform human living, it is this: the sense that actions have consequences, that what we say and do determines who we are. Our sheer humanity and how we express it in our actions and relationships actually matters. This is true for everyone though sometimes religious people behave as though they have first dibs, or a hotline to heaven. Surely religious practice needs to reflect how important the human project is. What we believe about God can only build on this. Christianity should rejoice in this insight: after all it claims to hold up the example of Jesus to its adherents and to be driven by the teaching of the Beatitudes. And these advocate just the kind of directness and integrity envisioned by the psalm.

And so to the promise of paradise

The Christian gospel holds up an unlikely representative of these virtues: someone on whom we cannot possibly pass any kind of judgment because we do not have the facts. Jesus tells a story about the ultimate destiny of those very differing characters: a rich man and the poor man who took up residence outside his front door.

> There was a rich man who was dressed in purple and fine linen and who feasted sumptuously every day. And at his gate lay a poor man named Lazarus, covered with sores, who longed to satisfy his hunger

with what fell from the rich man's table; even the dogs would come and lick his sores. The poor man died and was carried away by the angels to be with Abraham. The rich man also died and was buried. In Hades, where he was being tormented, he looked up and saw Abraham far away with Lazarus by his side. He called out, 'Father Abraham, have mercy on me, and send Lazarus to dip the tip of his finger in water and cool my tongue; for I am in agony in these flames.'

(Luke 16:19-24)

No explanation is offered. We have no way of knowing why the unnamed rich man was destined for hell while Lazarus made it safely to Abraham's bosom. The point of the story is revealed at the end: the rich man wants someone who has actually died to explain what is going on to the living relations he has left behind. 'If someone goes to them from the dead, they will repent', he claims. As he sees it, the baffling mystery of what lies beyond death can only be explained by someone who has made it through the experience. But the character named as Father Abraham in this account is clear: 'If they do not listen to Moses and the prophets, neither will they be convinced even if someone rises from the dead' (Luke 16:31). True understanding is only granted to those who listen and are open to the idea of life in a space beyond what is immediately apparent, or paradise. Is this what Lazarus learnt as the dogs licked his sores and comforted him?

When the Christian gospels tell us that God is revealed in the person of Jesus, the meaning of his words to the character known as the 'good thief' becomes apparent. At the very end of his own life, indeed from the cross where he was dying, Jesus defended a total stranger, the man who was hanging beside him. 'Truly, this day you will be with me in paradise.' Why?

What was important about this particular individual? What did he represent? After all he was a common criminal by all accounts and getting his just deserts. Yet Jesus defended him because he spoke the truth. When their fellow criminal, the other man who is crucified along with Jesus, shouts out, 'Are you not the Christ? Save yourself and save us', this man rounds on him: 'we indeed have been condemned justly, for we are getting what we deserve for our deeds, but this man has done nothing wrong.' Then he said, 'Jesus, remember me when you come into your kingdom' (Luke 23:40-42). The promise he receives is absolute: Jesus replied, 'Truly I tell you, today you will be with me in Paradise.'

This promise of paradise is given to a frail, very ordinary human being, someone who is a known criminal because, when it mattered, he told the truth. The lies around him were dismantled by the clarity of his conviction. He leaned into the truth and the truth in turn set him free.

This freedom is what is offered by all our attempts to live the life of paradise. It brings with it the gift of eternal life, of immortality. When we relegate heaven to the afterlife, we condemn ourselves to one-dimensional living.

The Wisdom

The association of the skies above us with heaven; of the present with the future is not accidental. Rather it is a telling reminder that we have a perspective on things. We matter; our opinions and values matter, and they affect other people too. How we live, who we care for, the truths we choose to tell all make a difference. In a strange way we have the capacity to create heaven for those around us, as indeed for ourselves.

Afterword

The many locations examined in the book all have a kind of application.

Obviously, they are physical places. We have all visited gardens, dreamed of climbing mountains, or looked up into a night sky. We have been exposed to fresh running water, warmed our hands on radiators, even enjoyed a trip on a boat – while carefully avoiding any confrontation with a whale. We relish the safety provided by the various city walls provided by our skin, our homes, our nationalities.

We know what these places look like and how being in them can affect how we feel. But there is more to life than understanding how we fit in our particular physical context. Beyond our sense of place, a whole world of wisdom and understanding opens up when you also think beyond the obvious.

Thinking about the places and stories explored here can help us understand more about the space we inhabit in the world and within our relationships. Reflecting on them while using Bible stories as a kind of lens to distil their inner message, as this book has tried to do, what emerges? Put simply, beyond place, there is space. There is a world of meaning to be uncovered as wide and as broad as any revealed by planetary exploration. Galaxies of meaning wait to be discovered by the intrepid questioner, by the person who is prepared to look beyond what is immediately apparent in the certainties – political, social, religious – pedalled by the custodians of untruth who rule our worlds.

Go beyond what you are told, beyond the received wisdom that worked yesterday. Every time you look up at the sky you are reminded that there is space to consider the emotional and spiritual value of human living and to reflect on the consequences of what you believe. If a new kind of God enters the frame at any point, do not be alarmed. The people whose stories appear in this book did not shy away from such an encounter – nor need you.

And this day perhaps you too will find yourself in paradise.

We pray to the God of infinite space.
Teach us to seek your truth in what we see and
what we cannot see.
Lift our imaginations to find you.
And when we come to die, may we rest in the
true space where we most truly belong.
This Easter, help us to rest in you.
Amen.

Action

- Make another photo of the pot where you planted a seed earlier. Has it grown? Have you?

A Place of Belonging

- Try reading the whole of Gerard Manley Hopkins' 'God's Grandeur'. Do you experience a desire to see 'the dearest freshness' he describes?

  The world is charged with the grandeur of God.
  It will flame out, like shining from shook foil;
  It gathers to a greatness, like the ooze of oil
  Crushed. Why do men then now not reck his rod?
  Generations have trod, have trod, have trod;
  And all is seared with trade; bleared, smeared with toil;
  And wears man's smudge and shares man's smell: the soil
  Is bare now, nor can foot feel, being shod.

  And for all this, nature is never spent;
  There lives the dearest freshness deep down things;
  And though the last lights off the black West went
  Oh, morning, at the brown brink eastward, springs —
  Because the Holy Ghost over the bent
  World broods with warm breast and with ah! bright wings.

  > Gerard Manley Hopkins: *Poems and Prose*
  > (Penguin Classics, 1985)

- When did you last read the Beatitudes? Do you find them a useful way of evaluating human attitudes as a pathway to the 'reward of heaven'?

  Blessed are the poor in spirit, for theirs is the kingdom of heaven.
  Blessed are those who mourn, for they will be comforted.

The Heavens are Telling

Blessed are the meek, for they will inherit the earth.
Blessed are those who hunger and thirst for
 righteousness, for they will be filled.
Blessed are the merciful, for they will receive mercy.
Blessed are the pure in heart, for they will see God.
Blessed are the peacemakers, for they will
 be called children of God.
Blessed are those who are persecuted for
 righteousness' sake, for theirs is the kingdom of
 heaven.
Blessed are you when people revile you and
 persecute you and utter all kinds of evil against
 you falsely on my account. Rejoice and be glad,
 for your reward is great in heaven, for in the
 same way they persecuted the prophets who
 were before you.

(Matt. 5:3–10)

- What do you think the words are when the heavens 'tell the glory of God'? Try saying,

The heavens are telling the glory of God;
and the firmament proclaims his handiwork.
Day to day pours forth speech,
and night to night declares knowledge.
There is no speech, nor are there words;
their voice is not heard;
yet their voice goes out through all the earth,
and their words to the end of the world.
In the heavens he has set a tent for the sun,
which comes out like a bridegroom from his
 wedding canopy,

A Place of Belonging

and like a strong man runs its course with joy.
Its rising is from the end of the heavens,
and its circuit to the end of them;
and nothing is hidden from its heat.

(Ps. 19:1-6)

- Then listen to Joseph Haydn's setting from his Oratorio of 1801. It is called *The Creation* and is easily available online. The lyrics are given here:

The Heavens are telling the glory of God,
The wonder of his work displays the firmament.
Today that is coming speaks it the day,
The night that is gone to following night.
The Heavens are telling the glory of God,
The wonder of his work displays the firmament.
In all the lands resounds the word,
Never unperceived, ever understood.
The Heavens are telling the glory of God,
The wonder of his work displays the firmament.

- Finally, try Faure's 'In Paradisum' from his setting of the Requiem Mass. Roll these words around your tongue:

In paradisum deducant te angeli:
in tuo adventu suscipiant te martyres,
et perducant te in civitatem sanctam Jerusalem.
Chorus angelorum te suscipiat,
et cum Lazaro quondam paupere,
aeternam habeas requiem.

The Heavens are Telling

- Then read the English translation:

  May the angels lead you into paradise:
  may the martyrs receive you as you arrive,
  and bring you into the holy city of Jerusalem.
  May the choir of angels receive you,
  and with Lazarus, once a beggar,
  may you have eternal rest.

- Finally – of course – notice how you feel. Which are you most like: Lazarus – who begged at the gate of a rich man – or the repentant thief? Either way, heaven is your destiny. And Easter is a little heaven – a season of hope and belonging.

Acknowledgments

So many people have helped me write this book.

The expertise and good cheer of Nick Quinn, Robert Wright, Joan McBride, Jane McBride and Angela Tilby cannot go unacknowledged.

Added to which David Moloney of Darton, Longman and Todd has been generous with his encouragement and support.

To all of them: thank you and, as William Tyndale wrote in his prologue to the first New Testament in English,

'That we cal gospel is a greke word, and signyfyth good, mery, glad and joyful tidings, that maketh mannes hert glad, and makyth hym synge, daunce and leepe for joy.'

May this Lent and the season of Easter that follows bring you many occasions to sing, dance and, eventually, to leap for joy.